I0007919

Exam PL-900
Simplifying Microsoft
Power Platform
Fundamentals
By

Dr Issa Ngoie

Microsoft certifications hold significant value in the IT industry for several reasons:

1. **Industry Recognition**: Microsoft is a leading technology company, and its certifications are recognized and respected globally. Holding a Microsoft certificate demonstrates your expertise and proficiency in specific Microsoft technologies and platforms.

2. **Validation of Skills**: Microsoft certifications validate your knowledge and skills in using Microsoft products, technologies, and platforms. They provide tangible proof to employers and colleagues that you have the necessary expertise to perform specific job roles or tasks effectively.

3. **Enhanced Career Opportunities**: Microsoft certifications can enhance your career prospects by making you more marketable to potential employers. Many organizations prioritize candidates with Microsoft certifications, as they indicate a higher level of competence and dedication to professional growth.

4. **Expanded Knowledge and Skills**: Preparing for and obtaining a Microsoft certification requires comprehensive studying and practical experience. This process enhances your knowledge and skills, deepening your understanding of Microsoft technologies and enabling you to tackle complex challenges more effectively.

5. **Competitive Advantage**: In a competitive job market, having a Microsoft certification can give you an edge over other candidates. It demonstrates your commitment to continuous learning and professional development, making you a more desirable candidate for job opportunities.

6. **Networking and Community**: Microsoft certifications provide access to a vast network of certified professionals and an active community. Engaging with this community can offer opportunities for knowledge sharing, collaboration, and professional networking, enabling you to stay connected with industry trends and best practices.

7. **Skill Standardization**: Microsoft certifications establish a standardized skill benchmark across the industry. Employers can rely on these certifications to assess the skills and competencies of candidates, making the hiring process more efficient and effective.

8. **Professional Growth and Confidence**: Obtaining a Microsoft certification can boost your professional confidence and self-esteem. It demonstrates your commitment to personal growth, validates your expertise, and provides a sense of achievement in your career.

9. **Access to Microsoft Resources**: Microsoft provides a wealth of resources, including documentation, training materials, and support, to certified professionals. This access enables ongoing learning and skill development, keeping you updated with the latest advancements in Microsoft technologies.

10. **Continued Relevance**: Microsoft regularly updates its certification programs to align with evolving technology trends and industry demands. By maintaining your certification, you can stay current with the latest advancements and ensure your skills remain relevant in a rapidly changing IT landscape.

Certification details

Exam PL-900

Whether you're a beginning technical professional, student, or business user, this certification will prove your knowledge in the business value and product capabilities of Microsoft Power Platform. Create simple Power Apps, connect data with Microsoft Dataverse, build a Power BI Dashboard, automate a process with Power Automate, or build a chatbot with Power Virtual Agents.

Obtaining a certification on the PL-900 exam, also known as the Microsoft Power Platform Fundamentals, can offer several benefits. Here are some reasons why you might consider getting certified on Exam PL-900:

1. **Validation of Knowledge and Skills**: By passing the PL-900 exam and earning the certification, you demonstrate your understanding and proficiency in the Microsoft Power Platform. It serves as a validation of your knowledge and skills in working with Power Apps, Power Automate, Power BI, and Power Virtual Agents.

2. **Enhanced Career Opportunities**: Having a certification in the Power Platform can enhance your career prospects. It can make you stand out among other job candidates and increase your chances of landing job roles that involve developing, administering, or utilizing the Power Platform. Certification can help open

doors to new job opportunities or advance within your current organization.

3. **Industry Recognition**: Microsoft certifications are globally recognized and respected in the industry. Holding a certification on Exam PL-900 showcases your commitment to professional development and your dedication to staying up-to-date with the latest technologies and tools.

4. **Increased Credibility**: Certification adds credibility to your profile and demonstrates your expertise in the Power Platform. It provides employers, clients, and colleagues with confidence in your abilities and can help establish you as a subject matter expert in this domain.

5. **Access to Microsoft Certification Community**: Earning a certification on Exam PL-900 grants you access to the Microsoft Certification community, which includes forums, discussion groups, and resources. This community allows you to connect with other certified professionals, share knowledge, and gain insights into best practices and emerging trends.

6. **Foundation for Advanced Certifications**: The PL-900 certification serves as a foundational certification for more advanced certifications in the Microsoft Power Platform. It can be a stepping stone for pursuing higher-level certifications that focus on specific areas within

the Power Platform, such as app development, data analysis, or automation.

7. **Personal Growth and Development**: Studying for and passing the PL-900 exam can expand your knowledge and skills in the Power Platform. It provides an opportunity for personal growth and development, allowing you to enhance your understanding of these technologies and improve your ability to apply them effectively in real-world scenarios.

Power Platform Fundamentals refers to the foundational knowledge and understanding of the Microsoft Power Platform. The Microsoft Power Platform is a suite of tools and technologies that empower users to build custom business applications, automate workflows, analyze data, and create chatbot experiences.

The Microsoft Certified: Power Platform Fundamentals certification could be a great fit for you, if you'd like to:

➤ Demonstrate knowledge in building solutions with Microsoft Power Platform.
➤ Show familiarity in automating basic business processes with Power Automate and in creating simple Power Apps experiences.
➤ Highlight familiarity in performing data analysis with Power BI and in building practical chatbots with Power Virtual Agents.

Exam PL-900

It is recommended to have familiarity with computer technology, data analytics, cloud computing, and the internet. This fundamentals certification can serve as a steppingstone for anyone interested in advancing to other certifications.

To ensure you are prepared for the exam, we recommend:

➤ Fully understanding the skills measured.
➤ Studying the relevant self-paced content on Microsoft Learn or signing up for an instructor-led training event.
➤ Taking the free Practice Assessment to validate your knowledge and understanding of the exam experience.
➤ Shadowing a person on your team who works with Microsoft Power Platform.

What's next?

Register for your exam! After you pass the exam and earn your certification, celebrate your certification badge and skills on social platforms such as LinkedIn. To find out more, visit: use and share certification badges.

Depending on your goals, you may choose to go deep with advanced role-based certifications or take other fundamentals certifications once you earn this certification. The Power Platform training and certification guide can help you identify the right certifications for you.

Important

The English language version of this certification will be updated on June 22, 2023.

FUNDAMENTALS CERTIFICATION
Microsoft Certified: Power Platform Fundamentals

Skills measured

> - This list contains the skills measured on the exam required for this certification. For more detailed information, visit the exam details page and review the study guide.
> - Describe the business value of Microsoft Power Platform
> - Identify foundational components of Microsoft Power Platform
> - Demonstrate the capabilities of Power BI
> - Demonstrate the capabilities of Power Apps
> - Demonstrate the capabilities of Power Automate
> - Demonstrate complementary Microsoft Power Platform solutions

Job role:
> - Business User
> - Functional Consultant
> - Student

Exam PL-900

Contents

Exam PL-900

Exam PL-900

Exam PL-900

Exam PL-900

CHAPTER 1

THE BUSINESS VALUE OF THE MICROSOFT POWER PLATFORM

Modern businesses run on data. Daily, users are performing tasks such as entering their time for payroll, working through existing processes, or using data to make business related decisions. In our technology driven world, users can be empowered to gain insights from and interact with data all while automating menial or repetitive job tasks. Microsoft Power Platform enables your business to craft solutions while empowering you to unite customized technology to help everyone, from CEO to front line workers, and to drive the business with data-driven insights.

➢ Examine Microsoft Power Platform
➢ Describe the business value of the Power Platform
➢ Explore connectors in Power Platform
➢ Review using Microsoft Dataverse to organize business data

Exam PL-900

➢ Examine how Power Platform works together with Microsoft 365 apps and services
➢ Explore solutions using Power Platform Microsoft Teams
➢ Describe how Power Platform works with Dynamics 365
➢ Describe how Power Platform solutions can consume Azure Services
➢ Explore how Power Platform apps work together to create solutions

Microsoft Power Platform

The Power Platform provides organizations with the opportunity to empower their team members to build their own solutions through an intuitive low-code or no-code set of services. These services help simplify the process of building solutions. With Power Platform, solutions can be built in days or weeks, as opposed to months or years. Microsoft Power Platform is composed of five key products: Power Apps, Power Automate, Power BI, Power Virtual Agents, and Power Pages.

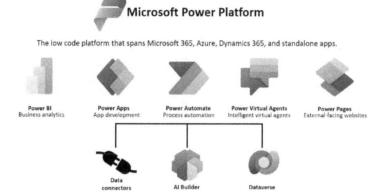

Microsoft Power Platform

The low code platform that spans Microsoft 365, Azure, Dynamics 365, and standalone apps.

| Power BI Business analytics | Power Apps App development | Power Automate Process automation | Power Virtual Agents Intelligent virtual agents | Power Pages External-facing websites |

Data connectors | AI Builder | Dataverse

Power Apps

Power Apps provides a rapid low code development environment for building custom apps for business needs. It is a suite of apps development services with a scalable data platform (Microsoft Dataverse) and an ability to interact with cloud & on-premises data sources. Power Apps enables the creation of web and mobile applications that run on all devices.

People use mobile apps for every area of their lives, and business should be no exception. Most out-of-the-box solutions do not meet exact business needs or integrate well with other business programs. Power Apps eases users into app development with a simple interface, so that every business user or pro developer can build custom apps.

Power Automate

Exam PL-900

Power Automate lets users create automated workflows between applications and services. It helps automate repetitive business processes such as communication, data collections, and decision approvals. Do not waste important productive hours on drafting the same email for a weekly update or manually walking through approval processes, Power Automate can provide automation not only for the individual user, but also for enterprise-grade process automation. Its simple interface allows users with every technical competence (from beginners to seasoned developers) to automate work tasks.

Power BI

Power BI is a business analytics service that delivers insights for analyzing data. It can share those insights through data visualizations, which make up reports and dashboards to enable fast, informed decisions. Power BI scales across an organization and has built-in governance and security, to allow businesses to focus on using data more than managing it.
You can consider Power BI as the analysis and insights leg of The Power Platform. A Power BI dashboard could potentially replace a standing meeting to report on company metrics such as sales data, progress against goals, or employee performance.

Power Virtual Agents

Power Virtual Agents enables anyone to create powerful chatbots using a guided, no-code graphical interface. It minimizes the IT effort required to deploy and maintain a custom solution by empowering subject matter experts to build and maintain their own conversational solutions. Power Virtual Agents is part of The Power Platform, so integration into Microsoft or third-party systems could be streamlined with Power Automate and its rich ecosystem, comprising hundreds of connectors. Users can enable chatbots to perform an action, by simply calling a Power Automate flow, which helps users to automate activities or integrate with back-end systems.

Power Pages

Microsoft Power Pages is a secure, enterprise-grade, low-code software as a service (SaaS) platform for creating, hosting, and administering modern external-facing business websites. Whether you are a low-code maker or a professional developer, Power Pages enables you to rapidly design, configure, and publish websites that seamlessly work across web browsers and devices. Power Pages provides you with rich customizable templates, a fluid visual experience through a reimagined design studio and an integrated learning hub to quickly build sites that suit your unique business needs.

Power Pages is the newest member of the Microsoft Power Platform family. With Power Pages, you can build sites by using the same shared business data stored in <u>Microsoft Dataverse</u> that you use for building apps, workflows, intelligent virtual agents, reports, and analytics with other Power Platform components in your organization.

In addition to the products listed above, there are additional tools that enhance the solutions you create on the Power Platform. Some of these are:

> **AI Builder** allows users and developers to add AI capabilities to the workflows and Power Apps they create and use. AI Builder is a turnkey solution that allows you to easily add intelligence to your workflows or apps and predict outcomes to help improve business performance without writing code.
> **Microsoft Dataverse** is a scalable data service and app platform which lets users securely store and manage data from multiple sources and integrate that data in business applications using a common data model to ensure ease and consistency to users. Microsoft Dataverse is the common currency that enables the components of Power Platform to work together. It's the foundation that enables the consolidation, display, and manipulation of data.
> **Connectors** enable you to connect apps, data, and devices in the cloud. Consider connectors as the bridge across which information and

commands travel. Connectors can be used by Power Apps, Power Automate flow, and logic apps. There are more than 900 pre-built connectors for Power Platform, enabling all your data and actions to connect cohesively. Examples of popular connectors include Salesforce, Office 365, Twitter, Dropbox, Google services, and more.

Now that we've introduced you to the primary elements of the Microsoft Power Platform, let's examine how the Power Platform provides business value to organizations.

The business value of the Power Platform

Many organizations struggle with building solutions that help their users be successful. Not only do they struggle trying to modernize their systems, but they simply don't have the resources required to meet the ever-changing needs of businesses today. With demands for targeted applications at an all-time high and labor shortages, it isn't uncommon to see application demand up to five times what departments can realistically deliver.

This demand for applications and resources isn't the only challenge facing enterprises today. As the

Exam PL-900

business climate changes, new factors are impacting businesses.

These impacts include:

> **Changing workforce expectations:** As millennials and Gen Z come to represent most of the workforce, organizations need to adapt to fit the way they work. They've grown up in a world of tailored experiences and collaborating through social media. To best apply their abilities, organizations need to be able to deliver more custom, streamlined, and collaborative digital experiences.
> **Increased costs for custom application development:** Building custom applications is time consuming and expensive. Not only do you need to factor in the costs to initially custom develop an application, but you need to factor in the costs to maintain it.
> **Need to become more agile:** Historically, solutions can take months to build and roll out. Once deployed, it can take weeks to implement every minor change. We no longer have that luxury. Business strategies and needs change rapidly, so organizations need to be able to quickly build solutions based on those changing needs.
> **Need to scale development efficiently:** To meet ever changing needs, organizations need to change how they develop solutions. By

responsibly enabling citizens developers (power users) as part of development processes, we can create hybrid development teams that empower the entire organization to grow.

The Power Platform makes it easy for organizations to address all the challenges mentioned. The combination of low code tools, along with the ability to use enterprise level application development tools, provides a collaborative solution. Citizen developers and professional developers can work together to build targeted solutions, based on needs of the people who use these applications every day.

For example, technicians in the field may encounter scenarios in which they need a mechanical part to execute a job. Ideally if that part is in inventory, they can easily request the part so they can continue to work. However, many times, there's a bottleneck in this process. Often, the technicians would need to first submit a request. This delay means waiting for the person in charge of the inventory to get back to them, only to find out later that the part isn't in stock.

This delay could be easily solved by building a dedicated app using Power Apps. By being able to check inventory levels while onsite, technicians don't have to spend time waiting to determine if the part is available. Not only can they see the inventory, but they can also easily request any part as needed. Since the technicians best understand what they need to complete the job at hand, they can use their first-hand knowledge to build out a prototype of the application using Power Apps. Technicians can dictate what reflects the best user interface and overall experience. This process is something that the developer traditionally starts. However, by providing the technicians with the ability to create a functional app, they can easily get started with a working concept. Once the prototype is built, professional developers can then fill in any potential gaps that go beyond the technician's technical ability. The professional developers can create the APIs that do the real-time checking of the company's inventory system. The APIs can be easily added to Power Apps and Power Automate. This collaborative approach to creating solutions is often referred to as fusion development, allowing organizations to use the best resources for the required task.

The image provides an example of the fusion development approach.

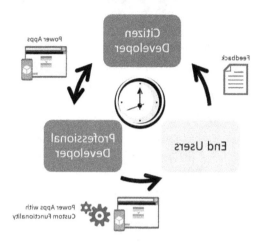

Using a low code/no code approach minimizes the amount of time that development resources spend working on items like screens, automations, and more. This efficiency frees them up to focus on the more advanced portions of the solution where their skills are more appropriately used. With over 900 prebuilt connectors, Power Platform helps to simplify integration with both internal and external systems. These connectors mean that organizations don't need to build custom integration solutions from the ground up, which can be costly to maintain.

In addition to cost benefits, the Power Platform helps to increase performance and efficiency. The flexibility of the platform lets you build applications and solutions that meet your business initiatives and goals. For example, a dedicated time management Power App could be quickly created to ensure that everyone is capturing their time on projects the same way. This means that the potential for data entry errors would be dramatically reduced. Integrated approvals that are built on Power Automate ensure that items are being automatically routed to the right person. Time off requests, for instance, can then be approved or rejected as quickly as possible.

Power Platform helps organizations build solutions that meet their ever-changing needs. Power Platform increases business agility by allowing organizations to quickly build applications in hours or days, as opposed to weeks or months. This speed of development ensures that by the time the solutions are created, it is still something that provides value. The business value typically extends improvement in multiple value drivers, such as performance improvement, direct/indirect cost savings, risk mitigation, and business transformation.

The speed of app development allows organizations to have a library of applications to facilitate day-to-day operations. These apps might include solutions for frontline worker scenarios like facilities management back-office administrative solutions like personnel management and employee onboarding, and many more.

Connectors and Microsoft Dataverse

Typically, when organizations are building business solutions, how the solution will work and perform can be impacted by several factors. Two of those areas are connecting to data sources and managing business data. Power Platform includes two tools that make these areas easier. They are data connectors and Microsoft Dataverse. Data connecters make it easy to connect to data across different services. Microsoft Dataverse is a business database that not only stores business data, but also includes other built-in features such as security and more.

Let's take a moment and examine each of these elements a little more closely.

Connectors

Creating solutions that span multiple services can create challenges. One of those challenges is ensuring that you can perform the necessary operations in all systems. The challenge is that you need to be access the service with a valid account, but that the account needs to be able to perform the necessary actions across all services. Let's look at the following document processing example.

A building management uses vendors to perform services at their buildings, such as cleaning properties after tenants leave and providing landscaping services at their properties. After the jobs are completed, vendors send invoices to the building management company. The building management company may want to automate processing invoices from vendors.

Currently the process is as follows:

> ➢ Invoices are received as email attachments. The management company uses Microsoft Exchange for processing emails.
> ➢ These attachments are downloaded and stored in Microsoft SharePoint.
> ➢ Each invoice is sent to a specific person for approval. Approval is made in Microsoft Teams.
> ➢ Once approved, the invoices are entered into the company's ERP system. The management company uses Oracle.
> ➢ Once entered, a confirmation email with the invoice number must be sent back to the vendor.

Automating a process like this requires interaction with multiple services. There are likely different accounts being used with each service, and different data operation that are being executed. In this example, we would be working with at least four different services.

> ➢ **Office 365 Outlook:** First, you would need to monitor a specific Microsoft Exchange mailbox.
> ➢ **Microsoft SharePoint:** Attachments are downloaded and saved to a specific folder in Microsoft SharePoint.
> ➢ **Microsoft Teams:** Invoice approval requests are sent to managers in Microsoft Teams,

where they can either approve or deny the request.

➤ **Oracle:** Once approved, the new invoice is created in Oracle. Details of the invoice are stored so they can be used alter.

➤ **Office 365 Outlook:** A confirmation email is sent using a dedicated mailbox to the company that submitted the invoice.

With Power Platform, data connectors make working with different data sources easier. They act as the bridge between data sources and your app or workflow. Power Platform has more than 900 connectors available to various data sources. Connectors also include a series of actions that simplify the process of working with those data sources. For example, the Office 365 Outlook connector has prebuilt actions for working with mailboxes, such as downloading attachments, and sending emails, managing events, and more. When using a connector, you just need to provide some basic details about the action you want to complete. Data connectors are used throughout Power Platform. For example, in Power Apps, they are used to connect apps to data. A company might create an order fulfillment application for their employees who work in the field. Data connectors would be used to connect the app to data sources like an SQL database or Microsoft Dataverse. In Power Automate, data connectors can be used to connect to data sources that are used as either triggers or actions.

Microsoft Dataverse

Microsoft Dataverse allows organizations to securely store and manage data used by your business applications. Dataverse data is stored in tables. A table is a set of rows and columns. Each column in a table stores specific type of data such as names, locations, ages, dates, salaries, and so on. In addition to data storage, Dataverse also has other elements that help with securing data, data validation, and productivity.

Each Dataverse instance includes a base set of standard tables that cover typical business scenarios such as accounts, contacts, and activities. This base set of tables reduces the amount of time that it takes for organizations to start building solutions since there are already standard business tables available. Additionally, organizations can also create custom tables specific to their needs and populate them with data.

For example:

> ➤ A real estate company might create tables to store the properties they sell, represent open houses, or store showings.
> ➤ A financial company might add tables to represent loan applications or bank accounts.
> ➤ An auto repair company might add tables to represent the parts they sell or the services they provide.

Once the tables are created, application makers can use tools like Power Apps to build rich business applications that use this data. For example, a real estate company might create a property management application for their agents working in the field. The app would provide agents with access to the properties stored in Dataverse.

Using Dataverse provides these benefits:

> - **Easy to manage**: Both the metadata and data are stored in the cloud.
> - **Easy to secure:** Data is securely stored so users can only access what they need to. Role-based security allows you to control access to tables for different users within your organization.
> - **Rich metadata**: Data types and relationships are used directly within Power Apps.
> - **Logic and validation**: Define calculated columns, business rules, workflows, and business process flows to ensure data quality and drive business processes.
> - **Productivity tools**: Tables are available within the add-ins for Microsoft Excel to increase productivity and ensure data accessibility.

Many solutions built on Power Platform use both Dataverse and connectors heavily. Dataverse acts as the primary business data storage mechanism, and connectors are used in the different apps and

Exam PL-900

automations that are connecting to different data services.

Now that we have introduced you to some of the primary elements of Power Platform, let's see how it can be used with other services.

How Power Platform works with Microsoft 365 apps and services

Organizations around the world use Microsoft technologies in the enterprise capacity. They often use Microsoft 365 for as their email and productivity platform. They might also use SharePoint as their document management platform. Because of the pervasive use of Microsoft 365 services, there are multiple built-in scenarios where the Power Platform can help you to create a more streamlined solution by interacting directly with Microsoft 365 services.

Power Platform includes multiple connectors that are designed to work with Microsoft 365 services.

Just a few of the connectors available include:

> Office 365 Outlook
> Office 365 Users
> Excel
> SharePoint

Administrators, managers, and end users can use these connectors to help be more productive. During any given day, a typical end user can receive more than 100 emails. Many of those incoming emails have attachments that need to be saved somewhere, such as a SharePoint site or a OneDrive for Business folder. With Power Platform, a user could easily create a Power Automate flow that monitors their inbox for incoming emails with attachments. When attachments are detected, the flow could locate the appropriate customer folders in SharePoint and automatically save the attachments there. If that process manually takes one to two minutes and is being done 20 to 30 times per day, this illustration alone could save up to 2 hours a week. This is just one of many examples.

Many organizations still use Microsoft Excel to run entire departments. Excel's formula capabilities and the ability to create elements such as Charts and Pivot tables make it easy for managers to keep track of daily items. Unfortunately, getting data into Microsoft Excel is often a manual process consisting of copying and pasting data from different applications into Excel. In some cases it needs the user to manually enter the data. In some industries, end users spend five to 10 hours a week just entering data into Excel. With the personal productivity automation tools available from the Power Platform, end users can automate the process of capturing this data and entering it into Excel. Power Automate Desktop flows mimics the keystrokes and mouse clicks on behalf of the user. Now, data entry tasks that took minutes could take seconds, freeing the users to work on other items.

There are just some of the many different examples of where Power Platform can be used with Microsoft 365 apps and services.

How Power Platform works with Microsoft Teams

When COVID-19 hit the world, organizations were forced to rethink how their work force gets things done. Many organizations switched their workers to work remotely. This introduced a need for better collaborative tools organizations can utilize.

Microsoft Teams has filled that need for many organizations. It provides a central point where users can collaborate with other users, have meetings, manage projects, and more. One key advantage of Microsoft Teams is how extensible and adaptable it is. This means organizations can build custom applications for Teams based on the needs of their users. Microsoft Power Platform is the innovative gateway to rapidly build Teams compatible apps using low-code attributes. All Power Platform components can be used with Microsoft Teams.

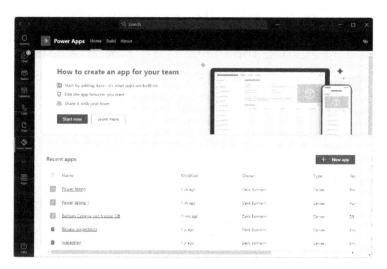

Let's examine them in a little more detail.

> **Power BI:** The Power BI tab for Microsoft Teams adds support for reports in the Teams workspace and allows users to share interactive Power BI content and collaborate with others in Teams channels and chats. You can create packaged Power BI app content from scratch and distribute it as an app or create a template app in Power BI. Additionally, use the new Power BI app in Teams to bring your entire basic Power BI service experience into Teams.

> **Power Apps:** The Power Apps app in Teams provides an integrated experience for app makers to create and edit apps and workflows within Teams. They can quickly publish and

share the apps to team members. The members can use the apps without having to switch between multiple apps and services. For example, a company might create an incident reporting application that can be accessed directly from Microsoft Teams. When a user needs to report an incident, they can do so without ever needing to leave Microsoft Teams.

> **Power Automate:** You can create flows to automate repetitive work tasks directly within the Teams environment with the Power Automate app in Teams. You can trigger a flow from any message in Microsoft Teams and use Adaptive Cards within Power Automate. Additionally, you can build flows to customize and add further value to Microsoft Teams from within the new Power Apps app in Teams.

> **Power Virtual Agents:** The Virtual Agents app in Teams lets you create, manage, and publish conversational chatbots easily from within Teams. You can share your bots with other people in your organization to chat and get answers for their questions.

> **Dataverse for Teams:** Dataverse for Teams is a built-in low-code data platform for Microsoft Teams that empowers users to build custom apps, bots, and flows directly in Microsoft Teams using Power Apps, Power Virtual Agents, and Power Automate.

> **Virtual Assistant for Teams:** Virtual Assistant is a Microsoft open-source template that

enables you to create a robust conversational solution while maintaining full control of user experience, organizational branding, and necessary data. You can configure your virtual assistant for integration into the Teams environment.

Let's look at an example.

Since the global pandemic hit in 2020, real estate companies have dramatically changed how they do business. First, all their real estate agents are remote workers now. Most of them come into the office once a month at the most. Since a majority of their workforce is mobile, being able to collaborate with team members is more important than ever. Their agents spend most of their day working in Microsoft Teams. It is important that they not only collaborate with other employees, but also perform day-to-day activities. By leveraging Power Platform with Teams, we can provide real estate agents with the following:

> Dedicated Power Virtual Agent bots embedded in Microsoft Teams can be used to field by agents to field questions they might have, as well as help them with day-to-day tasks. For example, a chat bot could answer questions about open house protocols, as well as assist agents with scheduling open houses.
> A dedicated expense submission app could be built using Dataverse for Teams to help agents

submit expenses related to travel, staging, and open houses right for Teams.

➢ Power BI reports that provide analytics around properties can be easily embedded inside Microsoft Teams.

In the image, we can see a dedicated chat bot inside Microsoft Teams that helps answer agents' questions related to different things such as open house scheduling protocols.

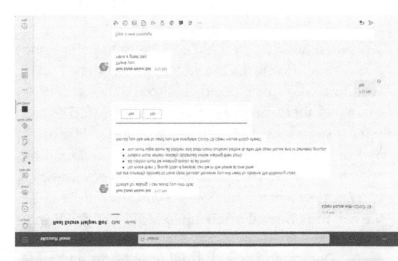

How Power Platform works with Microsoft Dynamics 365 apps

Exam PL-900

Dynamics 365 is a set of intelligent business applications that help organizations run their entire business and deliver greater results through predictive, AI-driven insights. From Finance and Intelligent Order Management to Sales and Customer Service, Dynamics 365 has a variety of enterprise resource planning (ERP) and customer engagement applications.

There are many ways that the Power Platform works with Dynamics 365 products. First, all Dynamics 365 customer engagement apps are what are referred to as model-driven applications. Model-driven applications are built using Power Apps. They are based on a data model store within Microsoft Dataverse. Components such as forms, views, charts, and dashboards are used to present data to end users.

Model-driven applications are not the only component of the Power Platform used by Dynamics 365 applications. Other Power Platform components used by Dynamics 365 customer engagement apps can include:

> **Power BI:** The business analytics capabilities provided by Power BI are often used to connect to Dynamics 365 applications and provide important insight into an organization. These visualizations can then be used inside

Dynamics 365 apps such as Dynamics 365 Sales, or Customer Service.

> **Power Automate:** Items called business process flows are the primary component in Dynamics 365 customer engagement apps. They help provide a guide for people to get work done. For example, Dynamics 365 Sales includes business process flow that helps guide sellers beginning with a lead and ending with a closed sale.

> **Power Virtual Agents:** Intelligent chatbots are becoming a regular part of customer support organizations. They can help to answer specific customer questions and deflect cases away from agents to reduce their workload. Dynamics 365 Customer Service can provide support across multiple channels to easily direct incoming phone calls, SMS, or Facebook messages to Power Virtual Agent bots first. The bot can then escalate to a live customer service agent working in Dynamics 365 Customer Service, as needed.

> **Power Pages:** Many organizations provide customers with self-support options where customers can access a portal and find answers to questions, engage with support, or even open new support tickets. Power Pages makes it easy for organizations to create externally facing sites that connect to Dataverse that customers can access.

Exam PL-900

The image shows an example of a Power BI dashboard displaying work order data that was automatically created using the Visualize in Power BI feature that is built into model-driven applications such as Dynamics 365 Field Service.

How Power Platform solutions consume Microsoft Azure services

The Azure cloud platform consists of hundreds of products and cloud services designed to help you bring new solutions to life to solve today's and future challenges. These services range from data storage services to virtual machines, to artificial intelligence services. Microsoft Azure service provides you with the opportunity to build, run, and manage

Exam PL-900

applications across multiple clouds, on-premises, and at the edge, with the tools and frameworks of your choice.

Power Platform and Azure services are a perfect complement for each other, and the possibilities for using them together are endless. Azure services can be used with Power Platform to help modernize legacy systems, automate processes, and create advanced analytical solutions.

Let's look at an example of how an organization might use Azure and Power Platform.

The example demonstrates how you can deploy portals to automate manual or paper-based processes and surface a rich user experience. Employ Azure API management and Azure Functions to connect custom APIs, which tap into your legacy systems. By using Azure-managed databases and a low-code approach to automate tasks, you can lower the overall solution costs. You can quickly build apps that are real-time, resilient, and scalable.

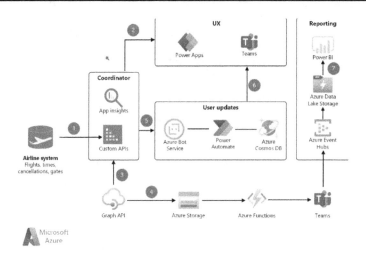

The data flows through the solution as follows:

1. The airline system communicates with a custom API hosted in <u>Azure API Management</u>.
2. A custom API coordinator receives notifications and handles incoming messages from the airline system, assigning flights to Microsoft Teams channels and sending them to <u>Power Apps</u>.
3. When a user selects a flight to monitor, or when the system assigns the user to a flight, the system queues a Graph API call in an Azure Storage Account queue for further processing.
4. <u>Azure Functions</u> runs the Graph API calls based on the incoming messages in the storage queue, sending notifications to

Teams, and also streams all events to an <u>Azure Event Hubs</u> for further analytics.

5. The airline's notification system is managed by a custom bot messaging service that employs <u>Azure Bot Service</u>.
6. Custom bots send flight updates to users in Teams.
7. An <u>Azure Data Lake</u> storage offers long-term retention and micro-batch processing of events from Event Hubs, ultimately generating insightful reports with Power BI.

How Microsoft Power Platform apps work together

Power Platform can add value to any business by helping you to analyze, act, and automate. Act by building custom apps in Power Apps, automate processes based on the data you collect in Power Automate, and analyze the data you have collected in Power BI.

Consider a business that has IT equipment for general use. Currently, equipment check-out is conducted by visiting the IT office, checking if the product is available, then writing your name with the equipment type in a notebook. Employees may have to visit IT several times before equipment becomes available, and IT personnel must drop their tasks to personally check on the equipment status or collect it for the employee. Sometimes employees hold onto the equipment for longer than they intend, and IT personnel spend time tracking it down. In addition, important equipment information such as serial numbers and warranty details are kept somewhere else in the IT office. How can Power Platform improve this process?

Power Apps allows us to build an app that has all equipment listed, the status of that equipment, and even important details such as use instructions. With their phone or tablet, employees can check out the available equipment then walk to IT at a specified pickup time, where the equipment will be ready along with all the necessary notes. Power Automate can read when equipment needs to be returned and send reminder emails to the employees. Users can see when equipment is booked through the app and request check-out for a future date. Power BI can take all the data generated from the app and analyze it to help your IT leaders understand what equipment is used most often and by whom. This way you can decide if you need to purchase additional equipment, if some users or departments need dedicated equipment, and when your equipment has reached the end of its usefulness.

This is only one common scenario in which Power Platform can transform the way businesses operate.

To expand on this a little more, let's look at another example. Consider a real estate company that has a team of agents who work in the field meeting with potential sellers and showing properties to buyers. In addition to their agents, they also have a team of managers who are there to support their agents.

The real estate company's agents need the following:

> Quickly search for active property listings while in the field.
> Easily intake new properties when working with new sellers including capturing property details, snap pictures, and schedule open houses as needed.

The real estate company's managers need to be able to do the following:

> Easily see which properties are currently listed.
> Ensure that property inspections are conducted as needed.
> Access important details such as how many offers have been made on a property and manage any incoming offers.
> Easily identify similar properties in the area.
> Have a singular area where they can analyze the current landscape of properties, they are

selling, and drive business decisions based on those actions.

Additional information:

> ➤ The real estate company uses Microsoft Outlook as their primary email application.
> ➤ They use Microsoft Teams. Real estate agents spend a large portion of their day working in Microsoft Teams.

Let's see how Power Platform could be used to create a tailored solution for our real estate company that provides everyone in their organization with the tools they need regardless of their needs.

Create a solution in Power platform

Now that you have seen a few different examples, consider your own business and what processes take up valuable time and are a burden to customers or employees. How can you use Microsoft Power Platform to improve them?

Real-world scenario

The Microsoft Power Platform offers significant business value in various real-world scenarios. Here's an example of how the Power Platform can provide tangible benefits to a business:

> **Scenario**: Streamlining Sales Processes A company wants to optimize its sales processes, improve efficiency, and enhance customer engagement. They decide to leverage the Microsoft Power Platform to achieve their goals.

1. **Power Apps**: The company uses Power Apps to create a custom sales application that streamlines the sales pipeline. Sales representatives can easily track leads, manage opportunities, and update customer information on-the-go using mobile devices. This improves productivity and ensures accurate and up-to-date data.

2. **Power Automate**: Power Automate is utilized to automate repetitive sales tasks and workflows. For example, when a new lead is created in the sales application, Power Automate can automatically trigger notifications to sales representatives, assign tasks, and send personalized follow-up emails to prospects. This reduces manual effort, increases responsiveness, and improves overall sales efficiency.

3. **Power BI**: The company leverages Power BI to gain insights into sales data. They create interactive dashboards and reports that provide real-time visibility into key sales metrics, such

as revenue, win/loss ratios, and sales performance. Sales managers can easily identify trends, analyze sales data, and make data-driven decisions to drive revenue growth.

4. **Power Virtual Agents**: To enhance customer engagement, the company builds a chatbot using Power Virtual Agents. The chatbot is integrated into their website and sales application, allowing customers to get immediate support, ask product-related questions, and receive personalized recommendations. The chatbot assists customers 24/7, improves response times, and increases customer satisfaction.

Business Value:

a. **Improved Sales Productivity**: By streamlining sales processes, eliminating manual tasks, and providing a centralized sales application, the company experiences increased sales productivity. Sales representatives can focus more on selling activities, spend less time on administrative tasks, and close deals faster.

b. **Enhanced Customer Experience**: The chatbot powered by Power Virtual Agents provides immediate and personalized support to customers, improving their overall experience. Customers receive quick responses to their queries, access relevant information, and feel more engaged with the company, leading to higher customer satisfaction and loyalty.

c. **Data-Driven Decision Making**: Power BI enables sales managers to gain insights from sales data, empowering them to make data-driven decisions. By analyzing key metrics and trends, they can identify areas of improvement, optimize sales strategies, and allocate resources effectively to drive revenue growth.

d. **Agility and Adaptability**: The Power Platform's low-code/no-code capabilities allow the company to quickly adapt to changing business needs. They can easily modify the sales application, automate new workflows, or enhance the chatbot without extensive coding or IT intervention. This agility enables the company to respond rapidly to market dynamics and stay competitive.

e. **Cost Savings**: The automation of sales processes and elimination of manual tasks result in cost savings. Sales representatives can focus on revenue-generating activities, reducing the need for additional resources. Additionally, the company saves on customer support costs by leveraging the chatbot for handling routine inquiries.

In this real-world scenario, the Microsoft Power Platform enables the company to streamline sales processes, enhance customer engagement, and make data-driven decisions. The business value includes improved sales productivity, enhanced customer experience, informed decision-making, agility, and cost savings, ultimately driving business growth and competitiveness.

GLOSSARY

Certainly! Here is a glossary of terms related to the business value of the Microsoft Power Platform:

1. ***Low-Code Development:*** Low-code development refers to a visual development approach that allows users to build applications and solutions with minimal coding. The Power Platform offers a low-code development environment, enabling business users and citizen developers to create custom applications and workflows without extensive coding knowledge.

2. ***Rapid Application Development (RAD):*** RAD is an agile software development methodology that emphasizes quick iteration and prototyping. The Power Platform's low-code capabilities facilitate rapid application development, enabling

faster delivery of business applications and solutions.

3. **Citizen Developer:** A citizen developer is a non-professional developer who creates applications or solutions using low-code or no-code platforms. The Power Platform empowers citizen developers to create business apps and automate processes without heavy reliance on IT or development teams.

4. **Data Integration:** Data integration refers to the process of combining and consolidating data from different sources into a unified view. The Power Platform allows seamless integration with various data sources, both within and outside the Microsoft ecosystem, enabling businesses to gain insights and automate processes based on consolidated data.

5. **Process Automation:** Process automation involves automating manual or repetitive tasks to improve efficiency and productivity. The Power Platform offers robust automation capabilities through Power Automate, allowing businesses to streamline workflows, trigger actions

based on events, and reduce manual effort.

6. **Power Apps:** Power Apps is a component of the Power Platform that enables users to build custom web and mobile applications without extensive coding. It provides a canvas-based development environment and a library of pre-built components to accelerate app creation.

7. **Power Automate:** Power Automate (previously known as Microsoft Flow) is a workflow automation tool within the Power Platform. It allows users to create automated workflows that integrate different systems and services, enabling seamless data exchange and process automation.

8. **Power BI:** Power BI is a business intelligence tool that enables users to visualize and analyze data through interactive dashboards and reports. It integrates with the Power Platform, allowing businesses to gain insights from data collected by Power Apps and automate actions based on data-driven insights.

9. Power Virtual Agents: Power Virtual Agents is a no-code bot development platform that allows users to create chatbots and virtual agents to interact with customers or employees. It empowers businesses to automate customer support, provide self-service options, and improve engagement through conversational interfaces.

10. **AppSource:** AppSource is Microsoft's marketplace for business applications, add-ins, and connectors. It provides a centralized platform for users to discover and acquire Power Platform solutions developed by Microsoft and its partners, expanding the capabilities and functionality of the Power Platform ecosystem.

These terms highlight the key components and benefits of the Microsoft Power Platform in driving business value through low-code development, process automation, data integration, and empowering citizen developers.

QUESTION AND ANSWERS

Q: How does the Microsoft Power Platform increase productivity?

A: The Microsoft Power Platform increases productivity by providing a low-code development environment that allows users to quickly create custom applications and automate processes. This eliminates the need for extensive coding and reduces the reliance on IT and development teams, empowering business users to build solutions themselves. With the Power Platform, businesses can streamline their operations, automate manual tasks, and improve overall efficiency.

Q: What advantages does the Power Platform offer in terms of agility and time-to-market?

A: The Power Platform offers agility and quick time-to-market by enabling rapid application development. Its low-code approach allows users to visually build applications, eliminating the need for traditional development cycles. Business users and citizen developers can create and iterate on applications quickly, responding to changing business needs and market demands faster than traditional development methods. This agility allows businesses to stay competitive and bring solutions to market more efficiently.

Exam PL-900

Q: How does the Power Platform contribute to cost savings?

A: The Power Platform contributes to cost savings in several ways. Firstly, the low-code development approach reduces the need for specialized development resources, enabling citizen developers and business users to create applications themselves. This reduces the reliance on IT and development teams, resulting in cost savings on development resources. Additionally, the Power Platform's scalability and flexibility allow businesses to leverage their existing investments and integrate with other Microsoft services and third-party applications, avoiding the need for costly redevelopments or system replacements.

Q: What role does data-driven insights play in the business value of the Power Platform?

A: Data-driven insights are a crucial part of the business value offered by the Power Platform. With integration capabilities and Power BI analytics, businesses can connect to various data sources, consolidate data, and gain valuable insights. Power BI's visualization and reporting capabilities enable users to analyze data and make informed decisions. This empowers businesses to identify trends, discover opportunities, and optimize processes, ultimately leading to improved performance and competitiveness.

Q: How does the Power Platform enhance collaboration within an organization?

A: The Power Platform enhances collaboration by bridging the gap between business users, IT professionals, and citizen developers. With its low-code development environment and visual tools, different stakeholders can work together more effectively to build applications and automate processes. The Power Platform encourages the sharing and reuse of solutions, fostering collaboration and knowledge exchange within the organization. By bringing teams together, the Power Platform promotes innovation and accelerates the development and deployment of solutions.

Q: What are the benefits of scalability and flexibility offered by the Power Platform?

A: The Power Platform provides scalability and flexibility to accommodate the needs of businesses of all sizes. Whether it's a small team or a large enterprise, the Power Platform can scale to meet the requirements. Additionally, the Power Platform allows businesses to integrate with other Microsoft services, such as Azure and Dynamics 365, as well as third-party applications, expanding the capabilities and functionality of the platform. This flexibility enables businesses to leverage existing investments, integrate systems, and build comprehensive solutions tailored to their specific needs.

Q: How does the Power Platform help in modernizing legacy systems?

A: The Power Platform helps in modernizing legacy systems by providing integration capabilities. Businesses can connect their legacy systems with new applications and services built on the Power Platform, leveraging existing investments and extending the functionality of their legacy systems. This approach allows businesses to adopt modern technologies and practices while preserving their previous investments. By integrating legacy systems with the Power Platform, businesses can enhance functionality, improve efficiency, and unlock new capabilities without the need for a complete system overhaul.

Q: What role does regulatory compliance play in the value of the Power Platform?

A: Regulatory compliance is an essential aspect of the Power Platform's value proposition. As part of the Microsoft ecosystem, the Power Platform aligns with Microsoft's robust security and compliance standards.

QUESTIONS

Certainly! Here are questions related to the business value of the Microsoft Power Platform:

1. How does the Microsoft Power Platform increase productivity?
2. What advantages does the Power Platform offer in terms of agility and time-to-market?
3. How does the Power Platform contribute to cost savings?
4. What role does data-driven insights play in the business value of the Power Platform?
5. How does the Power Platform enhance collaboration within an organization?
6. What are the benefits of scalability and flexibility offered by the Power Platform?
7. How does the Power Platform help in modernizing legacy systems?

8. What role does regulatory compliance play in the value of the Power Platform?

Feel free to ask for detailed answers to any specific questions!

CHAPTER 2

FOUNDATIONAL COMPONENTS OF MICROSOFT POWER PLATFORM

Microsoft Power Platform enables your business to craft solutions while empowering you to unite customized technology to help everyone, from the CEO to the front-line workers, drive the business with data. To understand how to begin creating solutions with the Microsoft Power Platform, it is important to understand some of the key foundational elements involved in creating solutions.

> ➢ Examine different Power Platform administrative options

Exam PL-900

➤ Describe security and governance in Power Platform
➤ Explore Microsoft Dataverse and how to use it to build business solutions
➤ Examine Power Platform connectors

Power Platform administration

Power Platform environments

In Power Platform, environments are used to store, manage, and share your organization's business data, apps, and flows. Each environment allows you to provision one Microsoft Dataverse database for use within that environment. Microsoft Dataverse environments allow you to manage user access, security settings, and the storage that is associated with that database.

Each environment is created under a Microsoft Azure Active Directory (Azure AD) tenant. Its resources can only be accessed by users within that tenant. An environment is also bound to a geographic location, like the United States. When you create a Microsoft Dataverse database in an environment, that database is created within datacenters in that geographic location. Any items that you create in that environment (including connections, gateways, flows that are using Power Automate, and more) are also bound to their environment's location.

You can create more than one environment to manage solution development and data storage by setting up one environment for development, another for testing, and another for production use. The development environment is for developers to create solutions. Once the solutions are ready for testing, they are moved to another environment called test. A separate environment ensures that everything can be tested without impacting users. Once the solution is ready, it can be moved to production. Also, you can set up an environment based on a geographical location. For example, you might set up an environment for Europe and another for Asia. Each of these environments has zero or only one instance of Microsoft Dataverse.

Administrative experiences

Microsoft Power Platform has a rich set of administrative experiences that can be used to administer the different aspects of your solution. From the Power Platform admin center, you can create new environments or manage security. From the maker portals you can manage Microsoft Dataverse. Depending on what you want to do, there's a targeted administrative experience for it. Let's examine the many different experiences available.

Exam PL-900

Microsoft Power Platform admin center

The Power Platform admin center (Https://admin.powerplatform.microsoft.com) is the primary administrative experience for the Microsoft Power Platform. The portal allows administrators to manage their environments and configure many of the primary settings for Power Apps, Power Automate, and customer engagement apps for Dynamics 365.

In the Power Platform admin center, settings are grouped into broad categories and are accessed by selecting the link on the left-hand side of the portal. These categories are:

- **Home:** Provides overall information, such as if there are any services disruptions, etc. Different cards can be added to better personalize this screen based on your needs.
- **Environments**: This section lists all the environments in this tenant. This includes Microsoft Dataverse environments and other environments such as Dataverse for Teams environments.
- **Analytics:** This section provides analytical details about Microsoft Power Platform such as Dataverse analytics, Power Automate Flow Statistics, and Power Apps details.

- **Billing:** The billing center contains details related to user licenses.
- **Settings:** This section lets you review and manage settings at a tenet level, such as being able to control who can create and manage the different types of environments available.
- **Resources:** This section is where you can view capacity statistics for your tenant and manage and install features related to Dynamics 365 applications.
- **Help + Support:** This section is where you can create new support requests and manage any existing requests that have been previously submitted.
- **Data integration:** This section lets you create or add predefined connections and monitor these connections between Microsoft Dataverse and other data stores like Salesforce or SQL Server.
- **Data:** This section is where you can manage the different data sources, on-premises data gateways, and virtual network data gateways associated with this tenant.
- **Policies:** This section is where you can manage some of the different data security policies and other security features, such as the Customer Lockbox and tenant isolation.

- **Admin Centers:** Provides access to the different admin centers that can impact Microsoft Power Platform solutions such as the Microsoft 365 admin center, Azure active directory and more.

Additional admin and maker portals

In addition to the Power Platform admin center, there are several different administrative experiences that can be used as part of Power Platform. Each experience is designed based on the product you are working with. For example, the primary experience that is used to make applications and manage the Dataverse instance associated with an environment is the Power Apps maker portal (Https://make.powerapps.com).

In the image, you can see an example of the maker portal displaying the different model and canvas applications that are currently deployed to this environment.

The Power Apps maker portal also provides for the following items:

> **Tables:** Allows you to manage the Microsoft Dataverse tables deployed in this environment. You can easily create new tables and perform tasks such as modifying the different forms, views, and relationships in the Dataverse instance.
> **Connections:** Allows you to manage the connections being used by apps in this environment.
> **Flows:** Provides access to any flows that have been created for this environment.
> **Chatbots:** Provides access to any chatbots that have been created for this environment.

- ➢ **AI Models:** Provides access to AI builder models for this environment.
- ➢ **Solutions:** Provides access to any Solutions that have been deployed to this environment.
- ➢ **Cards:** Provides access to Cards created in this environment.
- ➢ **Choices:** Allows you to manage the choice columns in this environment.
- ➢ **Connections:** Allows you to manage the connectors that are being used in this environment.
- ➢ **Dataflows:** Provides access to Dataflows being used in this environment.
- ➢ **Power Platform:** Provides access to other Power Platform Maker portals.

Items in the middle section can be pinned and displayed as needed. For example, if your organization isn't doing anything with Cards, you can choose to not have it displayed. If you access it, you can select more, which are then displayed displayed.

Each of the primary Power Platform components has a corresponding maker portal. The table provides a list of the different maker portals available:

Product	URL	Description
Power Automate	https://make.powerautomate.com	Used to create and manage the Cloud and Desktop flows deployed.
Power BI	https://app.powerbi.com	Used to create and manage Power BI reports and dashboards.
Power Virtual Agents	https://web.powerva.microsoft.com	Used to create intelligent chatbots that can be used by employees and customers.
Power Pages	https://make.powerpages.com	Used to create modern, secure business websites that can be used by employees and customers.

Explore the different portals

Now that we'e talked about the different administrative experiences available, let's see how to work with them. In the following video, we walk through some of the basic elements in the Power Platform admin center and introduce some of the other maker portals available.

Power Platform admin center

Power Platform security and governance

Organizations want to know that their data is not going to be compromised. For example, you don't want to accidentally pass through sensitive information in an application. The Power Platform service is governed by the Microsoft Online Services Terms and the Microsoft Enterprise Privacy Statement. For the location of data processing, refer to the

Microsoft Online Services Terms and the Data Protection Addendum.

The Microsoft Trust Center is the primary resource for Power Platform compliance information. Learn more at Microsoft Compliance Offerings.

The Power Platform service follows the Security Development Lifecycle (SDL). SDL is a set of strict practices that support security assurance and compliance requirements. Learn more at https://www.microsoft.com/securityengineering/sdl/practices.

Data loss prevention policies

Your organization's data is likely one of the most important assets you're responsible for safeguarding as an administrator. The ability to build apps and automation to use that data is a large part of your company's success. You can use Power Apps and Power Automate for rapid build and rollout of these high-value apps so that users can measure and act on the data in real time. Apps and automation are becoming increasingly connected across multiple data sources and multiple services. Some of these might be external, third-party services and might even include some social networks. Users generally have good intentions, but they can easily overlook the potential for exposure from data leakage to services and audiences that should not have access to the data.

Data loss prevention (DLP) policies act as guardrails to help prevent users from unintentionally exposing organizational data. DLP policies can be defined at the environment or tenant level, offering flexibility to craft sensible policies that strike the right balance between protection and productivity. Connectors can be classified as follows:

> **Business:** Connectors that host business -use data.
> **Non-****Business:** Connectors that host personal-use data.
> **Blocked:** Connectors that you want to restrict usage across one or more environments.

When a new policy is created, all connectors are defaulted to the **non-Business** group. From there they can be moved to **Business** or **Blocked** based on your preference. You can manage connectors when you create or modify the properties of a DLP policy from the Microsoft Power Platform admin center. These affect Microsoft Power Platform canvas apps and Power Automate flows.

Compliance and data privacy

Exam PL-900

Microsoft is committed to the highest levels of trust, transparency, standards conformance, and regulatory compliance. Microsoft's broad suite of cloud products and services are all built from the ground up to address the most rigorous security and privacy demands of our customers.

To help your organization comply with national, regional, and industry-specific requirements governing the collection and use of individuals' data, Microsoft provides the most comprehensive set of compliance offerings (including certifications and attestations) of any cloud service provider. There are also tools for administrators to support your organization's efforts. In this part of the document, we will cover in detail the resources available to help you determine and achieve your own organization requirements.

Data Protection

Data in transit between user devices and the Microsoft datacenters are secured. Connections established between customers and Microsoft datacenters are encrypted, and all public endpoints are secured using industry-standard TLS. TLS effectively establishes a security-enhanced browser to server connection to ensure data confidentiality and integrity between desktops and datacenters. API access from the customer endpoint to the server is also similarly protected. Currently, TLS 1.2 (or higher) is required for accessing the server endpoints.

Accessibility in Microsoft Power Platform

One of the things that Microsoft values the most is making sure that Power Platform is accessible and inclusive to all kinds of users all over the world. An accessible canvas app will allow users with vision, hearing, and other impairments to successfully use the app. In addition to being a requirement for many governments and organizations, following the below guidelines increases usability for all users, regardless of their abilities. You can use the Accessibility Checker to help review potential accessibility issues in your app. For more details and suggestions on making your canvas apps more accessible, visit Create accessible canvas apps in Power Apps.

Microsoft Dataverse

Microsoft Dataverse is a cloud-based solution that easily structures various data and business logic to support interconnected applications and processes in a secure and compliant manner. Managed and maintained by Microsoft, Dataverse is available globally but deployed geographically to comply with your potential data residency. It isn't designed for stand-alone use on your servers, so you need an internet connection to access and use it.

Dataverse is different from traditional databases in that it is more than just tables. It incorporates security, logic, data, and storage into a central point. It's designed to be your central data repository for business data, and you might even be using it already. Behind the scenes, it powers many Microsoft Dynamics 365 solutions such as Field Service, Marketing, Customer Service, and Sales. It's also available as part of Power Apps and Power Automate with native connectivity built right in. The AI Builder and Portals features of Microsoft Power Platform also utilize Dataverse.

The image shows a visualization that brings together the many offerings of Microsoft Dataverse.

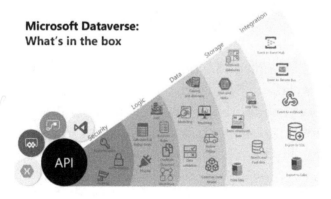

Here's a brief explanation of each category of features.

- ➤ **Security**: Dataverse handles authentication with Azure Active Directory (Azure AD) to allow for conditional access and multi-factor authentication. It supports authorization down to the row and column level and provides rich auditing capabilities.
- ➤ **Logic**: Dataverse allows you to easily apply business logic at the data level. Regardless of how a user interacts with the data, the same rules apply. These rules could be related to duplicate detection, business rules, workflows, or more.
- ➤ **Data**: Dataverse offers you the control to shape your data, allowing you to discover, model, validate, and report on your data. This control ensures your data looks the way you want regardless of how it is used.
- ➤ **Storage**: Dataverse stores your physical data in the Azure cloud. This cloud-based storage removes the burden of worrying about where your data lives or how it scales. These concerns are all handled for you.
- ➤ **Integration**: Dataverse connects in different ways to support your business needs. APIs, webhooks, eventing, and data exports give you flexibility to get data in and out.

As you can see, Microsoft Dataverse is a powerful cloud-based solution for storing and working with your business data. In the following sections, you look at Microsoft Dataverse from the lens of data storage for Microsoft Power Platform, where you start your journey. Keep in mind the other rich capabilities discussed which you can explore further as your usage increases.

To get started, Microsoft Dataverse lets you create one or many cloud-based instances of a standardized database. The database includes predefined tables and columns that store data commonly found across nearly all organizations and businesses. You can customize and extend what's stored by adding new columns or tables. The ease of setting up a Microsoft Dataverse database and standardized data model under it simplifies your ability to concentrate your efforts on building solutions without worrying about infrastructure, storage, and data integration. With your data stored in Microsoft Dataverse, there are many ways to access it. You can work with the data natively with tools such as Power Apps or Power Automate. Any business solution can connect to Dataverse using connectors APIs. With the power of features such as role-based security and business rules you can trust your data is safe no matter how it is accessed.

Scalability

A Dataverse database supports large data sets and complex data models. Tables can hold millions of items, and you can extend the storage in each instance of a Microsoft Dataverse database to four terabytes per instance. The amount of data that is available in your instance of Microsoft Dataverse is based upon the number and type of licenses that are associated with it. Data storage is pooled between all licensed users, so you can allocate storage as needed for each solution that you build. Incremental storage can be purchased if you need more storage than what is offered within standard licensing.

Microsoft Dataverse structure and benefits

The structure of a Microsoft Dataverse database is based upon the definitions and schema in the Common Data Model. The key benefit of using the Common Data Model as the basis of a Microsoft Dataverse database is that it simplifies the integration of solutions that use a Common Data Model schema. The standard tables of the solution are the same. You can take advantage of a rich ecosystem of solutions that vendors have built from using the Common Data Model. Best of all, there is practically no limit to how far you can extend a Microsoft Dataverse database.

Describe tables, columns, and relationships

A table is a logical structure containing rows and columns that represents a set of data. In the screenshot, you see the standard account table and various elements that can be managed as part of it.

Exam PL-900

Types of tables

The three types of tables are:

> **Standard** - Several standard tables, also known as out-of-box tables, are included with a Dataverse environment. Account, business unit, contact, task, and user tables are examples of standard tables in Dataverse. Most of the standard tables included with Dataverse can be customized.

> **Managed** - Tables that are not customizable and have been imported into the environment as part of a managed solution.

> **Custom** - Custom tables are unmanaged tables that are either imported from an unmanaged solution or are new tables created directly in the Dataverse environment.

Columns

Columns store a discrete piece of information within a row in a table. You might think of them as a column in Excel. Columns have data types, meaning that you can store data of a certain type in a column that matches that data type. For example, if you have a solution that requires dates, such as capturing the date of an event or when something occurred, then you store the date in a column with the type Date. Similarly, if you want to store a number, then you store the number in a column with the type of Number.

The number of columns within a table varies from a few columns to a hundred or more. Every database in Microsoft Dataverse starts with a standard set of tables, and each standard table has a standard set of columns.

Understand relationships

To make an efficient and scalable solution for most of the solutions that you build, you'll need to split up data into different containers (tables). Trying to store everything in a single container would likely be inefficient and difficult to understand.

The following example helps illustrate this concept.

Imagine that you need to create a system to manage sales orders. You'll need a product list along with the inventory on hand, the cost of the item, and the selling price. You also need a master list of customers with their addresses and credit ratings. Finally, you will need to manage sales invoices as well to store invoice data. The invoice should include information such as date, invoice number, salesperson, customer information including address and credit rating, and a line item for each item on the invoice. Line items should include a reference to the product that you sold and be able to provide the proper cost and price for each product and decrease the quantity on hand based upon the quantity that you sold in that line item.

Creating a single table to support the functionality in the above example would be inefficient. A better way to approach this business scenario is to create the following four tables:

> Customers
> Products
> Invoices
> Line items

Creating a table for each of these items and relating them to one another will allow you to build an efficient solution that can scale, while maintaining high performance. Splitting the data into multiple tables also means that you will not have to store repetitive data or support huge rows with large

Exam PL-900

amounts of blank data. Additionally, reporting will be much easier if you split the data into separate tables.

Tables that relate to one another have a relational connection. Relationships between tables exist in many forms, but the two most common are one-to-many and many-to-many, both of which are supported by Microsoft Dataverse.

Business logic in Microsoft Dataverse

Many organizations have business logic that impacts how they work with data. For example, an organization who is using Dataverse to store customer information might want to make a field such as and Identification number field required based on the type of customer they are. In Microsoft Dataverse, you build this logic using business rules. Business rules allow you to apply and maintain business logic at the data layer instead of the app layer. Basically, when you create business rules in Microsoft Dataverse, those rules are in effect regardless of where users interact with the data.

For example, business rules can be used in canvas and model-driven apps to set or clear values in one or many columns in a table. They can also be used to validate stored data or show error messages. Model-driven apps can use business rules to show or hide columns, enable, or disable columns, as well as create recommendations based on business intelligence.

Business rules give you a powerful way to enforce rules, set values, or validate data regardless of the form that is used to input data. Additionally, business rules are effective in helping to increase the accuracy of data, simplify application development, and streamline the forms presented to end users.

Below is an example of a simple, yet powerful use of business rules. The business rule is configured to change the field **Credit Limit VP Approver** to be a required field if the Credit Limit is set to greater than $1,000,000. If the credit limit is less than $1,000,000 then the field is optional.

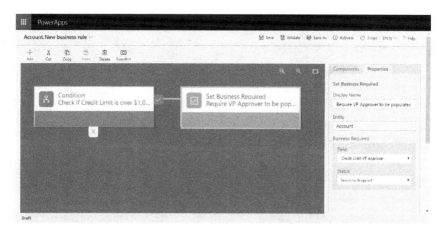

By applying this business rule at the data level instead of the app level, you have better control of your data. This can ensure your business logic is followed whether it is being accessed directly from Power Apps, Power Automate, or even via an API. The rule is tied to the data, not the app.

Working with dataflows

Dataflows are self-service, cloud-based, data preparation technology. Dataflows are used to ingest, transform, and load data into Microsoft Dataverse environments, Power BI workspaces, or your organization's Azure Data Lake Storage account. Dataflows are authored by using Power Query, a unified data connectivity and preparation experience already featured in many Microsoft products, including Excel and Power BI. Customers can trigger dataflows to run either on demand or automatically on a schedule, data is always kept up to date.

Because a dataflow stores the resulting entities in cloud-based storage, other services can interact with the data produced by dataflows.

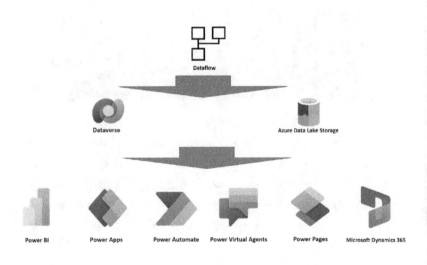

For example, Power BI, Power Apps, Power Automate, Power Virtual Agents, and Dynamics 365 applications can get the data produced by the dataflow by connecting to Dataverse, a Power Platform dataflow connector, or directly through the lake, depending on the destination configured at dataflow creation time.

The following list highlights some of the benefits of using dataflows:

> A dataflow decouples the data transformation layer from the modeling and visualization layer in a Power BI solution.
> The data transformation code can reside in a central location, a dataflow, rather than be spread out among multiple artifacts.
> A dataflow creator only needs Power Query skills. In an environment with multiple creators, the dataflow creator can be part of a team that together builds the entire BI solution or operational application.
> A dataflow is product agnostic. It's not a component of Power BI only, as you can get its data in other tools and services.
> Dataflows take advantage of Power Query, a powerful, graphical, self-service data transformation experience.
> Dataflows run entirely in the cloud. No additional infrastructure is required.

Exam PL-900

> You have multiple options for starting to work with dataflows, using licenses for Power Apps, Power BI, and Customer Insights.
> Although dataflows are capable of advanced transformations, they are designed for self-service scenarios and require no IT or developer background.

Power Platform connectors

Microsoft Power Platform is made powerful by its ability to use data across many platforms. To work across multiple data platforms, components of Microsoft Power Platform use connectors. You can think of connectors as a bridge from your data source to your app or workflow. This bridge allows information to be conveyed back and forth. Connectors allow you to extend your business solutions across platforms and add functionality for your users.

Data Sources

To understand the types of connectors and their capabilities, you must first understand the types of data sources to which they connect. The two types of data sources are tabular, and function based.

Tabular data - A tabular data source is one that returns data in a structured table format. Power Apps can directly read and display these tables through galleries, forms, and other controls. Additionally, if the data source supports it, Power Apps can create, edit, and delete data from these data sources. Examples include Microsoft Dataverse, SharePoint, and SQL Server.

Function-based data - A function-based data source is one that uses functions to interact with the data source. These functions can be used to return a table of data but offer more extensive action such as the ability to send an email, update permissions, or create a calendar event. Examples include Office 365 Users, Project Online, and Azure Blob Storage.

Both data source types are commonly used to bring data and incremental functionality to your solutions. As you can see, connecting to data sources allows you to integrate disparate parts of your business solutions to build them out cohesively. Now that you understand more about data sources, you're ready to learn about connectors.

Connectors are the bridges from your data source to your app, workflow, or dashboard. Microsoft Power Platform has more than 900 connectors available to common data sources. Connectors are divided into standard and premium. Some popular standard connectors are SharePoint, Outlook, and YouTube.

Premium connectors require additional licensing for your app and/or users. A few premium connectors are SQL Server, Survey Monkey, and Mail Chimp. The connector reference in the summary and resources unit lists all connectors and whether they are considered standard or premium. You can also use AppSource to source and install apps and use the connectors to non-Microsoft services.

Connectors can provide input and output between the data source and Power Platform, which can accelerate the delivery of Microsoft Power Platform business solutions. For instance, using Dynamics 365 apps such as Customer Service, you can set up Power Automate to notify users when specific customer types are added. Or you can use a SharePoint document library to store files that are fed into Power Apps to manage and distribute. Microsoft also provides connectors to their Azure services, providing advanced AI techniques to do tasks such as reading text off images or cognitive services like recognizing faces in images.

All Microsoft Power Platform business solutions can be used and implemented into Microsoft 365 apps such as Teams. This integration allows users to play Power Apps within Teams or run Power Automate from actions and events within Teams.

Triggers and Actions

Once you have established a data source and configured your connector, there are two types of operations you can use, triggers or actions.

Triggers are only used in Power Automate and prompt a flow to begin. Triggers can be time based, such as a Power Automate flow that begins every day at 8:00 am. They could be based off an action like creating a new row in a table or receiving an email. You always need a trigger to tell your workflow when to run.

Actions are used in Power Automate and Power Apps. Actions are prompted by the user or a trigger and allow interaction with your data source by some function. For example, an action would be sending an email in your workflow or app writing a new line to a data source.

Now that you understand what connectors are and how to use them, examine the different connectors available.

Standard Connectors

Standard tier connectors are connectors that are included in your standard Microsoft 365 subscription. Standard connectors cover many of the most used data sources such as SharePoint, OneDrive, and Power BI as well as third-party data sources such as Google Drive, Twitter, GitHub, and more.

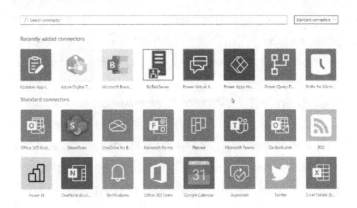

Premium Connectors

While standard connectors are available with a standard Microsoft 365 subscription, premium connectors are only available when you have the appropriate standalone plans such as Power Apps per user plan, or a Power Automate per user plan. The main advantage of premium connectors is that they allow you to connect to a larger number of services. Most premium connectors cover external applications such as Salesforce, DocuSign, Survey Monkey, Amazon, and so on. There are several Microsoft applications that use premium connectors such as Dynamics 365. Premium connectors are identified by the premium stamp.

Custom Connectors

If any of the over 900 connectors don't provide you with what you need, you can build a custom connector. Custom connectors allow you to extend your app by calling a publicly available API, or a custom API you are hosting in a cloud provider, such as Azure. API stands for Application Programming Interface and holds a series of functions available for developers. Connectors work by sending information back and forth across these APIs and gathering available functions into Power Apps or Power Automate. Because these connectors are function-based, they call specific functions in the underlying service of the API to return the corresponding data.

An advantage of building custom connectors is that they can be used in different platforms, such as Power Apps, Power Automate, and Azure Logic Apps.

You can create custom connectors using three different approaches:

Exam PL-900

> Using a blank custom connector
> From an OpenAPI definition
> From a Postman collection

While the requirements for each approach vary, they all require a Power Apps per app or per user plan. Each link above points to the instructions for each approach.

Note: The purpose of this module is to help you better understand data sources and connectors as a whole, but if you would like to learn more about custom connectors and even walk through an exercise to build one, check out the module **Use custom connectors in a Power Apps canvas app**.

Build a basic Dataverse data model

Contoso Real Estate wants to be able to keep track of the properties that they sell in Dataverse so the data can be easily used in canvas and model driven applications. To introduce you to how to build a table in Microsoft Dataverse, you're creating basic table in an existing Dataverse instance to store real estate properties.

The table includes five columns:

> Property Name

- ➤ Asking Price
- ➤ Bedrooms
- ➤ Bathrooms
- ➤ Client (This field is a lookup field that can either look up an Account or Contact.)

Important: This hands-on lab assumes that you have a Dataverse instance that you can work with. If you don't have an instance you can work with, you can obtain a 30-day Power Apps trial plan here.

1. Open a web browser and navigate to https://make.powerapps.com.
2. Using the navigation on the left, select **Tables**.
3. On the **Tables** screen, select **New Table**. On the menu that appears, select **New Table**.
4. Complete the table as follows:
   - ○ **Display Name:** Real Estate Property
   - ○ **Plural Name:** Real Estate Properties

New table ✕

Use tables to hold and organize your data. Previously called entities
Learn more

Properties   Primary column

Display name *

Real Estate Property

Plural name *

Real Estate Properties

Description

☐ Enable attachments (including notes and files) *

Advanced options ⌄

5. Select the **Primary columns** tab.

6. Change the **Display name** to **Property Name**.
7. Select the **Save** button to create the table. (It can take a few minutes for your table to be created.)

8. Once your table is created, under the **Schema** section, select **Columns**.
9. Select the **+ New Column** button.
10. Configure your new column as follows:
    o **Display name:** Asking Price
    o **Data Type:** Currency

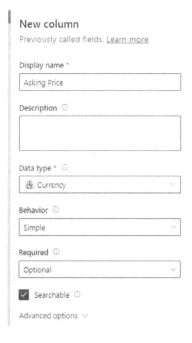

11. Select the **Save** button.
12. Select the **+ New Column** button again.
13. Configure your new column as follows:
    o **Display Name:** Bedrooms
    o **Data type:** Whole Number (Number > Whole Number)

New column

Previously called fields. Learn more

Display name *

Bedrooms

Description ⓘ

Data type * ⓘ

🔢 Whole number

Format *

🔢 None

14. Select the **Save** button.
15. Select the **+ New Column** button again.
16. Configure your new column as follows:
    - **Display Name:** Bathrooms
    - **Data type:** Whole Number (Number > Whole Number)

New column

Previously called fields. Learn more

Display name *

Bathrooms

Description ⓘ

Data type * ⓘ

🔢 Whole number

17. Select the **Save** button.
18. Select the **+ New Column** button again.
19. Configure your new column as follows:
    o **Display Name:** Client
    o **Data type:** Customer (Lookup > Customer)

New column

Previously called fields. Learn more

Display name *

Client

Description ⓘ

Data type * ⓘ

👥 Customer

Required ⓘ

Optional

20. Select the **Save** button.

Congratulations, you have successfully created a table in Dataverse. From this table, you can build forms and views based that could be used in model-driven applications, or you could connect to the table in a canvas application.

GLOSSARY

1. ***Power Apps:*** Power Apps is a low-code application development platform that allows users to build custom web and mobile applications. It provides a visual development environment with pre-built templates, drag-and-drop functionality, and data integration capabilities.
2. ***Power Automate:*** Power Automate (previously known as Microsoft Flow) is a workflow automation tool that enables users to create automated workflows across different applications and services. It allows for the seamless integration of data and actions, triggering processes based on events or specific conditions.
3. ***Power BI:*** Power BI is a business intelligence and data visualization tool that helps users analyze data and share insights through interactive dashboards

and reports. It allows for data exploration, real-time monitoring, and collaboration on data-driven decisions.

4. **Power Virtual Agents:** Power Virtual Agents is a no-code chatbot development platform that enables users to create conversational bots for various scenarios. It allows businesses to provide automated customer support, offer self-service options, and improve engagement through natural language interactions.

5. **Common Data Service (CDS):** The Common Data Service is a cloud-based data storage and management service that provides a unified and secure data platform for Power Platform applications. It allows for the creation, storage, and management of business data, ensuring consistency and interoperability across apps.

6. **Connectors:** Connectors are pre-built integrations that enable Power Platform applications to connect with external systems, services, and data sources. They provide a seamless way to bring in and interact with data from a wide range of sources, both Microsoft and third-party.

7. ***AI Builder:*** AI Builder is a component of the Power Platform that allows users to add artificial intelligence capabilities to their applications and workflows. It offers pre-built AI models for common scenarios such as text recognition, form processing, object detection, and prediction.

8. ***Data Connectors:*** Data connectors are specific connectors that facilitate the integration of Power Platform applications with various data sources. They enable users to connect to on-premises databases, cloud services, and applications, enabling data access and integration within Power Platform solutions.

9. ***Power Platform Admin Center:*** The Power Platform Admin Center is a centralized management portal that allows administrators to manage and govern the Power Platform within their organization. It provides control over environments, data policies, security settings, and user access.

10. ***Power Platform App Maker:*** The Power Platform App Maker is a role within the Power Platform that represents users

responsible for building and configuring applications. App Makers leverage the capabilities of Power Apps, Power Automate, Power BI, and other components to create customized solutions.

These foundational components form the building blocks of the Microsoft Power Platform, enabling users to develop applications, automate workflows, analyze data, and integrate with various systems and services.

QUESTIONS AND ANSWERS

Q: What is Power Apps, and how does it contribute to the Microsoft Power Platform?

A: Power Apps is a low-code application development platform that allows users to create custom web and mobile applications. It provides a visual development environment with drag-and-drop functionality and pre-built templates, enabling users to build apps without extensive coding knowledge. Power Apps integrates with other components of the Power Platform, such as Power Automate and Power BI, to create comprehensive solutions that streamline processes and enhance user experiences.

Q: How does Power Automate fit into the Microsoft Power Platform?

A: Power Automate is a workflow automation tool that enables users to create automated workflows across various applications and services. It allows for the seamless integration of data and actions, triggering processes based on events or specific conditions. Power Automate enhances the Power Platform by automating repetitive tasks, improving efficiency, and enabling the flow of information between different systems and services.

Q: What is the role of Power BI in the Microsoft Power Platform?

A: Power BI is a business intelligence and data visualization tool within the Power Platform. It allows users to connect to different data sources, create interactive visualizations, and share insights through interactive dashboards and reports. Power BI enables users to analyze data, gain valuable insights, and make data-driven decisions. It integrates with other

Exam PL-900

components of the Power Platform, such as Power Apps and Power Automate, to provide comprehensive data-driven solutions.

Q: How does Power Virtual Agents contribute to the Microsoft Power Platform?

A: Power Virtual Agents is a no-code chatbot development platform that allows users to create conversational bots. It enables businesses to automate customer support, provide self-service options, and improve engagement through natural language interactions. Power Virtual Agents integrates with other components of the Power Platform, allowing users to incorporate chatbots into their applications and workflows, enhancing the overall user experience.

Q: What is the Common Data Service (CDS) and its role in the Power Platform?

A: The Common Data Service (CDS) is a cloud-based data storage and management service within the Power Platform. It provides a unified and secure data platform for Power Platform applications. CDS allows for the creation, storage, and management of business data, ensuring consistency and interoperability across apps. It serves as a foundation for data integration and sharing within the Power Platform ecosystem.

Q: How do connectors contribute to the functionality of the Microsoft Power Platform?
A: Connectors are pre-built integrations that enable Power Platform applications to connect with external systems, services, and data sources. They provide a seamless way to bring in and interact with data from a wide range of sources, both Microsoft and third-party. Connectors enhance the functionality of the Power Platform by facilitating data integration, allowing users to access and utilize data from multiple systems in their applications and workflows.

Q: What is AI Builder, and how does it enhance the Power Platform?

A: AI Builder is a component of the Power Platform that allows users to add artificial intelligence capabilities to their applications and workflows. It offers pre-built AI models for common scenarios such as text recognition, form processing, object detection, and prediction. AI Builder enables users to leverage AI without extensive coding knowledge, making it easier to incorporate intelligent features into their Power Platform solutions.

Q: How does the Power Platform Admin Center support the management of the Power Platform? A: The Power Platform Admin Center is a centralized management portal that allows administrators to govern and manage the Power Platform within their organization. It provides control over environments, data policies, security settings, and user access. The Admin Center allows administrators to manage and monitor the usage and performance of Power Platform components, ensuring compliance, security, and effective governance of the platform.

QUESTIONS

Certainly! Here are questions specifically focusing on the foundational components of the Microsoft Power Platform:

1. What is Power Apps, and how does it contribute to the Microsoft Power Platform?
2. How does Power Automate fit into the Microsoft Power Platform?

3. What is the role of Power BI in the Microsoft Power Platform?
4. How does Power Virtual Agents contribute to the Microsoft Power Platform?
5. What is the Common Data Service (CDS) and its role in the Power Platform?
6. How do connectors contribute to the functionality of the Microsoft Power Platform?
7. What is AI Builder, and how does it enhance the Power Platform?
8. How does the Power Platform Admin Center support the management of the Power Platform?
9. What is the role of the Power Platform App Maker in the Microsoft Power Platform?

CHAPTER 3

HOW TO BUILD APPLICATIONS WITH MICROSOFT POWER APPS

Exam PL-900

Do you have inefficient or legacy business processes that you would like to modernize? Are you still moving information around using paper or even a shared Excel workbook? Do you want to be able to perform these business processes from different devices like PCs or mobile phones? Then you need Power Apps.

Power Apps is used to build apps that allow you to act on your data. Power Apps is great for replacing paper forms, legacy solutions, or just that spreadsheet that you and a few coworkers pass around. Using the skills and knowledge you already possess, you can build apps to interact with existing data by using more than 900 connectors. Once you build the apps on the web native Power Apps platform, they live in the cloud. The apps are easily shared and run on various platforms, including PCs, laptops, tablets, and mobile phones.

In this module, we will:

- ➤ Examine Power Apps
- ➤ Explore canvas applications
- ➤ Explore model-driven applications
- ➤ Differentiate between canvas and model-driven applications
- ➤ Build a basic canvas app
- ➤ Build a basic model-driven app

Exam PL-900

Power Apps

Power Apps is a no-code/low-code platform for building apps that builds off concepts like formulas in an Excel workbook such as SUM and TEXT. You can use Power Apps to build simple solutions like vehicle inspection forms and status reports, or complex business solutions for purchasing processes and inventory management. If you can envision an app to solve a business problem, then you can use your existing skills to build it. Although Power Apps can be used by virtually anyone, it also offers advanced functionality for seasoned developers to design complex applications with ease.

Work with your data where it lives

When organizations modernize a paper-based process, there are likely systems with data you can use. With Power Apps, you have choices. With hundreds of connectors, you can easily connect to data, using the underlying data service and app platform Microsoft Dataverse or a multitude of online and on-premises data sources.

Some common data sources include:

> ➢ Dataverse

Exam PL-900

- ➢ SharePoint
- ➢ Dynamics 365
- ➢ SQL Server and Azure SQL
- ➢ Office 365

You don't have to choose just one data source. Power Apps easily supports multiple data connections allowing you to bring data together from many platforms into a single app.

There are two primary application types that can be created with Power Apps: canvas and model-driven apps. Each application type has multiple features and functionality that helps support different scenarios. Let's look at each one in more detail.

Canvas applications

Most organizations have countless scenarios where people need assistance, need to perform some type of task, or have a duty that needs to be completed. For example, a nurse working at a hospital may need to triage a patient that is coming in for surgery. Another example could be a field technician who is working onsite at a customer location and finds that they do not have a specific part they need. It could also be as simple as an employee who is having an issue connecting to audio/video equipment in a conference room.

Typically, handling these scenarios might require many phone calls, multiple paper forms that need to be completed and passed along, and an extended wait time for processing. For example, the technician working in the field would often need to reach out to an inventory manager to identify if the part is in stock. The inventory manager likely needs to search in their inventory management software for the part. Depending on if they have the part or not, different forms need to be filled out so you can pull the part from inventory or order the part if needed. This process is not only requiring lots of environmental resources such as paper, but you have two people working on the issue.

Canvas apps created in Microsoft Power Apps are a great option for organizations to build tailored apps designed to perform specific tasks based on their needs. A key advantage to canvas apps is that they interact with data from multiple data sources. This means that you can integrate business data from a wide variety of Microsoft and third-party data sources into a single application. App designers can easily drag and drop a variety of different controls into their application, and then add the desired functionality by writing Power FX formulas. There are Excel-like expressions that help specify how to work with the data. Once created, canvas apps can be easily shared with users so they can run them in a browser or on a mobile device. Additionally, canvas can be embedded into SharePoint sites, Power BI reports, model-driven applications, or even Microsoft Teams.

Let's look at an example:

Heathrow Airport is one of the busiest airports in the world and models a small city in complexity and traffic. With over 76,000 people working on a given day and 200,000 travelers passing through, there's a strong need to continually optimize operations. One way to accomplish this goal is through the digitization of processes. They approached the process of digital transformation by empowering the frontline workers to build apps and solve problems. Through this process they have built at least 30 apps that have eliminated 75,000 pages of paperwork, reduced data entry by nearly 1,000 hours, and saved the airport hundreds of thousands of dollars.

Canvas apps are easy to create and a wonderful resource when you need a targeted application with a tailored user experience that integrates with multiple data sources. If you do not need a customer design and your data is in Microsoft Dataverse, you can automatically generate a model-driven app.

Let's see how Heathrow Airport uses Power Apps.

Heathrow Airport inspires employee engagement with Microsoft Power Apps

Model-driven applications

Unlike canvas apps where the app maker has control over the data sources, screen layout, and overall user experience, model-driven apps are always built from data in Microsoft Dataverse. Model-driven apps use a data first design, where app design focuses on adding components such as forms, views, charts, and dashboards to tables using an app designer tool. With model-driven apps, there's no need to worry about choosing the app size. They're responsive, which means that they work and display appropriately whether being accessed through a browser, a mobile phone, or tablet.

Model-driven applications are used as management applications. For example, when someone reports a problem with audio/visual equipment, they use a canvas application. To manage the incoming requests, assist users with troubleshooting, dispatch someone to fix them, and analyze overall operations related to the organization, organizations typically use a model driven app. Dashboards and charts let managers see overall performance such as how many issues are being reported and how they're being resolved. Support users can easily identify incoming requests and provide support directly from within the application.

You define the relationships, forms, views, business rules, and more at the data layer inside of the Dataverse. These definitions give you enough control to achieve the business result you're looking for without needing to write all the formulas yourself.

Here's an example of a fundraiser donations tracking model-driven app.

The fundraiser donations dashboard lets managers easily see details related to incoming donations based on different fundraisers the organization ran. Using the charts provided, managers can easily examine different donations based on the donation category, donation totals for each fundraiser, and even compare the actual donation totals vs the donation goals.

Additionally, they can easily create and manage fundraisers directly from the application and dive into each individual donation provided.

Between canvas apps and model-driven apps

How do you determine which app to use? If your application isn't going to be connected to a Microsoft Dataverse database, then the choice is easy. You create a canvas application since model-driven apps can only be built on top of Dataverse. Otherwise, it's important to first identify what your application is going to be used for.

The table provides a high-level comparison between the two.

	Canvas	Model-driven
Data source	Not Dataverse driven	Dataverse driven
App purpose	Task or screen focused	Back office / process focused
User Interface (UI)	Custom UI	Responsive / consistent UI
	Device integration	User personalization
	Easily embeddable	Data relationship navigation
		Security trimming of UI

To expand on this explanation a little more, let's look at an example. Contoso Real Estate sells commercial and residential properties. They have a team of agents in the field that meet with potential sellers and show properties to buyers. They need to quickly identify which properties to show based on the needs of the buyer they're working with. When working with a new seller, they also need to quickly intake the property, snap pictures, schedule open houses, and capture any other relevant information so the property can be listed as quickly as possible. Contoso's managers need to:

> ➢ quickly see which properties are currently listed
> ➢ know how many times they have been shown
> ➢ manage offers as they come in
> ➢ help provide support to sellers as they work to sell properties

From a seller standpoint, the best solution would be to create a canvas app to support them in the field. The canvas app can not only connect to Dataverse data, but it can easily connect to other data sources such as Google Calendar to schedule open houses for properties. The ability to create a custom user interface means the application can be designed to provide the best experience for sellers working in the field. Finally, because of the device integration capabilities, sellers can easily take pictures of the property using their mobile device, and those pictures are automatically associated with the property.

The image shows an example of what the seller's canvas application might look like.

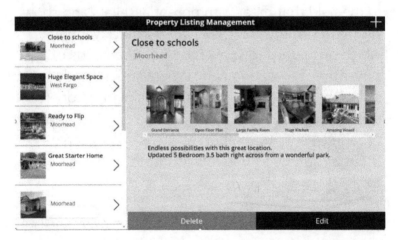

Sellers are provided with a list of properties they can easily search through to identify properties to show perspective buyers. Once a property is identified, they can easily view specifics about the property including pictures. This capability lets the buyer see the property and decide if it's worth visiting.

Let's take a closer look at how a canvas app can help listing agents be more productive while working in the field.

Canvas app

As far as the managers for Contoso Real Estate go, they need to have an application that lets them manage the big picture and help support sellers. A model-driven app would best help them support sellers and manage daily operations. As properties are entered by sellers using the canvas application, they're available in the model-driven app. Additionally, they would have easy access to open houses, showings, and offers that are stored in Microsoft Dataverse. Items like business rules and business process flows can be used to help guide sellers through the various processes: listing a home, staging the home, managing open houses and showings, and negotiating offers.

The image shows an example of what a model driven application might look like.

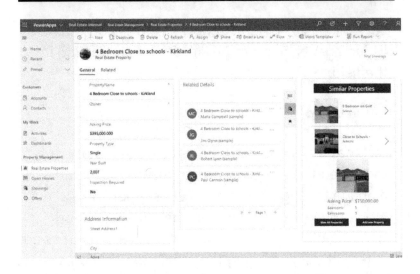

Under the Property Management group, managers can easily access things like the real estate properties that are currently for sale. As they open a specific property, they are presented with basic information such as the property type, asking price, and the year built. In the **Related Details** section, we have access to any open houses, showings, and offers associated with this property. This provides managers with everything associated with this property from a single screen without needing to navigate to different areas of the application.

Additionally, a canvas application can be used to help compliment the data in the model-driven application. In this case, we have an embedded canvas application on the Real Estate Property form. This app looks at the address, square footage, number of bedrooms, and asking price of the home being looked at. The app also lists similar properties in the surrounding area.

This information helps managers do things such as evaluate the asking price of the home vs similar properties in the area. If needed, they can adjust their asking price as needed.

Let's see how a model-driven application can help Contoso Real Estate better support their agents in the field to sell properties faster.

Model-driven app

As you see, when building solutions with Power Apps it's often about identifying what users are going to need an application to do, and then designing the applications accordingly. Most often, a solution contains a combination of both canvas and model-driven apps.

Now that we've discussed canvas and model-driven apps and explored scenarios for each of them, let's take a deeper look at how to build each of them.

Build a basic canvas app

The basic Power Apps creator journey to build a canvas app looks something like this:

> Identify a business need that can be addressed by Power Apps.
> Connect to any necessary data in your Power Apps.

> ➤ Design the app using controls, buttons, and an easy-to-use interface. Then your end user can interact with the data to accomplish the business need.
> ➤ Save and publish the app and test functionality.
> ➤ Once satisfied, share the app with end users to give them a better business process.

To help app creators during their journey, Power Apps has many different components to build solutions including screens, inputs, galleries, forms and more.

Let's review some of the most common elements you need to get started.

Power Apps Studio

Power Apps Studio is the web interface used to build Power Apps. With Power Apps, there's no client to download or install for building apps. Everything is done from the browser by logging into https://make.PowerApps.com. Once in Power Apps studio, you can create an app from scratch, or use one of the many different templates available to speed up development of your app.

Exam PL-900

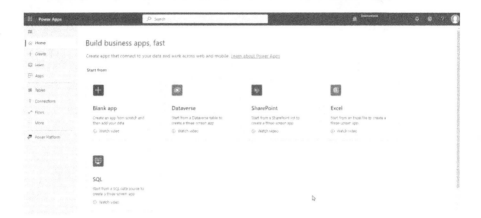

App format

The first step in creating your app is to choose the format of your app: Mobile or Tablet. While both formats can be used interchangeably on a mobile device, a tablet, or a computer, each has different defaults around sizing of the screens and controls. Once you choose the format for an app, you can't change it.

Connectors

Once you have identified the app format you want to use, you need to connect your app to your data. In Power Apps, this step is done using Connectors. There are over 900 prebuilt connectors available.

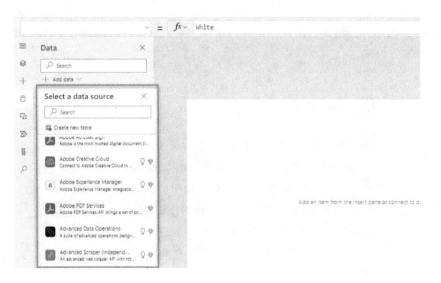

Galleries

As you build your app, you will likely encounter scenarios where you need to display a list of records on a screen. In Power Apps, this is done with the Gallery control. A gallery displays rows from a table of data. The display of a row is then defined by a template, which you can customize to meet your needs. This process allows you to control which columns are shown and how they are formatted. Power Apps then applies this template automatically to every row in your data.

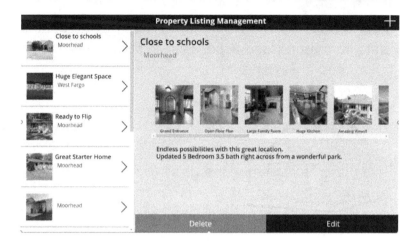

Forms

Unlike Galleries, Forms are focused on working with a specific record, often based on a selection from a gallery. In this experience, a user browses a gallery to find and select the desired row to view the details on the form. Forms enable a user to view detailed information, save new records and edit existing ones. The various actions performed with forms are controlled by form modes allowing the form to serve many purposes.

Input Controls

To allow you maximum flexibility in customizing your apps, Power Apps has a large selection of Input controls. Text inputs, buttons, dropdowns, toggles, date pickers, and sliders are a few examples. You can add these controls to galleries, forms, and screens to build a functional and aesthetic experience for your app. All inputs have a multitude of settings for default data, formatting, and actions which allow you to build an app that has the right user experience for your business process.

Intelligent Controls

In addition to common inputs as covered, Power Apps also provides a rich set of controls for more advanced operations. There are hardware-backed controls which allow access to the camera, bar code scanner, GPS, and more hardware features. There are also service backed controls like the business card reader or object detector which allow you to add artificial intelligence to your app without writing code.

Functions

Functions are the glue that binds all these controls, inputs, and data sources together. You can use one or more functions to create formulas in your apps. These formulas are like the language you use in Excel and can be used for actions such as sending data to a data source, formatting information, creating animations, and more. No complicated code is necessary. You just use powerful functions with straightforward inputs to enhance your app.

Now that we've walked through the process of building a canvas application, let's show you. In the following simulation, we connect to a data source to create an application. Once created, the app is easily modified based on our specific needs.

Click-through demo: Build a canvas app

In this click-through demonstration, you're guided through the process of creating a marketing segment that can be used with other features such as email marketing.

Build a canvas app

Build a canvas app

In this unit, you will generate a canvas app where the data source is a Microsoft Excel workbook that is stored in Microsoft OneDrive for Business. This Excel workbook has a table of different buildings owned by Contoso Manufacturing. Today, they must email the shared workbook between people as they travel to different locations to make updates. With a Power Apps canvas app, they will be able to view the buildings directly from their phones. In addition, they will also be able to edit the information and even add new buildings.

This example uses Excel, but keep in mind that you can use data from many other sources, including Microsoft Dataverse, Microsoft SharePoint, cloud services like Salesforce, and on-premises sources like

Exam PL-900

Microsoft SQL Server. This gives you the flexibility to build your app from your data no matter where it lives. You can also combine data sources within Power Apps to easily create associations between different data sources.

If you do not have a Power Apps account available, you can sign up for a free Power Apps Community Plan. This will allow you to learn and explore Power Apps in your own environment. For more information and to sign up, go to https://powerapps.microsoft.com/communityplan/

Connect to a data source

To connect to a data source, use the following procedure:

1. Download the Contoso-Site-Tracking.zip file, extract all of the files, and save them to your OneDrive for Business.
2. Go to https://make.powerapps.com and sign in with your organizational account.
3. In the left pane, select **Create**.
4. In the **Start from data** section, select **Excel**.
5. Under Connections, choose **OneDrive for Business**. If you don't have the connection available, click **New connection** to create one.

6. For **Choose an Excel file** on the right select the **Contoso Site Tracking.xlsx** file.
7. For **Choose a table** click **SiteInspector** and click **Connect**.

Power Apps will generate the app by inspecting your data and matching it with Power Apps capabilities so that you get a working app as a starting point. Generated apps are always based on a single list or table, but you can add more data to the app later.

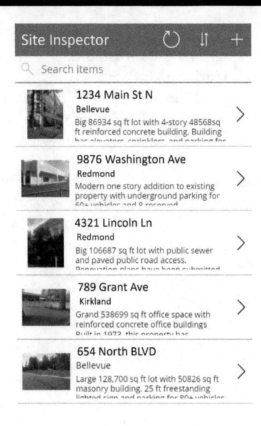

Explore the generated app

Your new three-screen app now opens in Power Apps Studio. All apps that are generated from data have the same set of screens that you can view from the Screens pane:

> **Browse screen** – This screen appears by default. In it, you can browse, sort, search, and

refresh the data from the data source. In the browse screen, you can add items to the data source by selecting the plus sign (+).

- ▪ **Note**
- ▪ It will be listed as BrowseScreen1 in the UI.

➢ **Details screen** - The details screen shows all the information about a single item. In this screen, you can open an item to edit or delete it.

Note

It will be listed as DetailScreen1 in the UI.

- • **Edit/create screen** - In this screen, you can edit an existing item or create a new one.

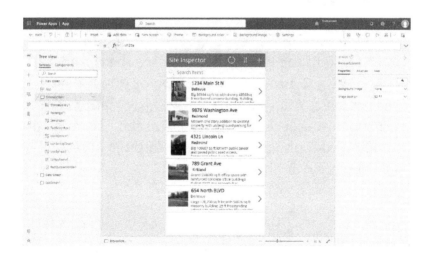

Exam PL-900

Select Play ▶ in the upper-right corner to practice using the app. Notice that it includes all the data from the table and provides a good default experience.

Now that you have generated the Contoso Site Tracking app you should take a few minutes to click through the app and explore its design. Take note of how you use a Gallery to browse the records from the Excel file. When you click on a record, you are taken to a different screen where a Form control displays the additional details. The app also includes the ability to edit those rows or even make a new row. This is a very functional app to build upon.

Once you have finished exploring the app, close out of preview mode by selecting the "X" in the upper-right corner. To make your app visible on the phone, it needs to be saved.

Saving your app

To save your app, select the **Save** button which is right next to the Play button. Replace the current title "App" with **Contoso Site Tracking app**, and then select **Save**. You will see a green check mark when all changes are successfully saved. You can now open the app on your phone. We will walk through accessing an app on your phone later.

Save as   ✕

This version of your app will be saved in the environment PL 900 Training

Name

Contoso Site Tracking App

Save   Cancel

Controls in Power Apps

A control is a UI element that produces an action or shows information. Many controls in Power Apps are like controls that you've used in other apps: labels, text-input boxes, drop-down lists, navigation elements, and so on. By leveraging controls, you can provide the user experience that best reflects what you want to deliver.

You can access Power Apps controls on the **Insert** tab.

A few common controls that can add interest and impact to your apps include:

> **Galleries** - These controls are layout containers that hold a set of controls that show rows from

a data source. These are commonly used when you want to display multiple records at a single time.

➢ **Forms** - These controls show details about your data and let you create and edit records.

➢ **Media** - These controls let you add background images, include a camera button (so that users can take pictures from the app), a barcode reader for quickly capturing identification information, and more.

➢ **Charts** - These controls let you add charts so that users can perform instant analysis while they're on the road.

To see what controls are available, select the **Insert** tab, and then select each option in turn.

The browse screen (BrowseScreen1)

Now that we have examined some of the controls available, let's examine how they are being used in our Site Inspection app. The first screen in the app is the browse screen, which is named BrowseScreen1 by default.

The browse screen has multiple controls. Controls in the browse screen that you'll want to become familiar with include:

> **BrowseGallery1** - This Gallery control takes up most of the screen and shows data from your data source.
> **NextArrow1** - When this Icon control is selected, it opens the details screen.
> **IconNewItem1** - Another Icon control that When selected, opens the edit/create screen.

The browse screen has multiple controls. Controls in the browse screen that you'll want to become familiar with include:

1. **BrowseGallery1** - This Gallery control takes up most of the screen and shows data from your data source.
2. **NextArrow1** - When this Icon control is selected, it opens the details screen.
3. **IconNewItem1** - Another Icon control that When selected, opens the edit/create screen.

Explore the details screen

The details screen is named **DetailScreen1** by default. Some of its controls are as follows:

1. **DetailForm1** - This control contains other controls and contains a data card for each column of the row that is being displayed.
2. **Address_DataCard1** - This is a card control. Each card represents a single column of the row. In this case, it shows the Address from the Site Inspector table, as shown in the previous unit.

3. **IconEdit1** - When this control is selected, it opens the edit/create screen so that the user can edit the current item.

Explore the edit/create screen

The third screen in the app is **EditScreen1**. Some of its controls include:

1. **EditForm1** - This control contains other controls and contains a data card for each column of the row that is being edited.
2. **Address_DataCard2** - This is a card control that shows the address from the Site Inspector table, as shown in the previous unit.
3. **IconAccept1** - When this control is selected, it saves the user's changes.

Install the app on your device

Power Apps can be used on mobile devices with the Power Apps mobile application. If you want to experience what it looks like on a mobile device, install the Power Apps Mobile app on your phone.

1. Download Power Apps Mobile from the app store for the platform that you want to use.
2. Sign in by using your username and password.
3. On your phone or tablet, run the **Contoso Site Tracking app** in Power Apps Mobile. If you do not want to install the app, you can run it in a browser.

If the app you are creating will be used on a mobile device, then it is a good idea to check how the Power App looks and runs on mobile so you can give your users the best experience.

Build a basic model-driven app

A model-driven app consists of several components that you select by using the App Designer. Components and component properties become the metadata. Let's look more closely at these components.

Data

The table shows the different data components that can make up a model-driven app, which can determine what data the app is based upon.

Component	Description
Table	Tables are items with properties that you track. Examples include contacts and accounts. Many standard tables are available. You can customize a non-system standard table (or production table). You can also create a custom table from scratch.
Column	Columns are properties that are associated with a table and help define that table. A column is defined by a data type, which determines the type of data that can be entered or selected. Examples of data types include text, number, date and time, currency, and lookup (which creates a relationship with another table). Columns are typically used in forms, views, and searches.
Relationship	Relationships define how tables can be related to each other. There are 1:N (one-to-many), N:1 (many-to-one), and N:N (many-to-many) relationships. For example, adding a lookup column to a table creates a new 1:N relationship between the two tables and lets you add that lookup column to a form.
Choice	This type of column shows a control that lets the user select among predefined options. Each option has a number value and a label. Choice columns can require either a single value or multiple values.

User interface

The table shows the user interface components, which determine how users interact with the app and what designer is used to create or edit the component.

Component	Description
App	Apps determine the app fundamentals, like components, properties, the client type, and the URL.
Site map	A site map specifies the navigation for your app.
Form	Forms include a set of data entry columns for a given table. A form can be used to create a new data row or edit an existing one.
View	Views define how a list of rows for a specific table appears in your app. A view defines the columns shown, the width of each column, the sorting behavior, and the default filters.

Logic

The logic components determine what business processes, rules, and automation the app has. Microsoft Power Apps makers use a designer that is specific to the type of process or rule they need.

Type of logic	Description
Business process flow	Business process flows walk users through a standard business process. Use a business process flow if you want everyone to handle customer service requests the same way. Or you can use a business process flow to require staff to gain approval for an invoice before submitting an order.
Business rule	Business rules apply rules or recommendation logic to a form to set field requirements, hide or show fields, validate data, and more. App designers use a simple interface to implement and maintain fast-changing and commonly used rules.
Flows	Power Automate is a cloud-based service that lets you create automated workflows between apps and services to get notifications, sync files, collect data, and more.

Visualization

The visualization components determine what type of data and reporting the app will show and which designer is used to create or edit that component.

Component	Description
Chart	Charts are individual graphical visualizations that can appear in a view or a form or that can be added to a dashboard.
Dashboard	Dashboards show one or more graphical visualizations in one place that provide an overview of actionable business data.
Embedded Microsoft Power BI	Power BI adds embedded Power BI tiles and dashboards to your app. Power BI is a cloud-based service that provides business intelligence (BI) insight.

Some examples of visualizations in a model-driven app:

Building model-driven apps

Model-driven apps are built using the App designer. It's a simplified user interface that allows you to specify which tables the app is based on and which visual elements should be included. Let's look at the App Designer for one of the available sample model-driven apps called "Fundraiser."

This application includes two Dataverse tables: Donation and Fundraiser.

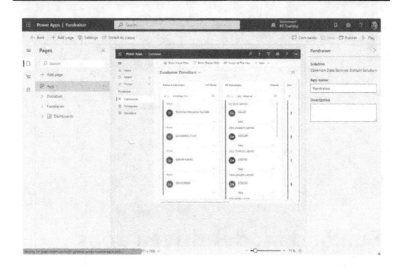

Once you've defined the tables for your app, you need to define the visual elements that are used to present the data to users. For each table, you need to specify the following information:

> **Forms** – Defines how users see and interact with individual records.
> **Views** – Defines how lists of rows are presented for each table. For example, you might create a view to display a list of all active fundraisers.

You can specify which specific forms or views to include for a table by selecting either the table form or view and choosing either **Manage forms** or **Manage Views**.

For example, the Account table in Dataverse will include all columns that have been defined for it.

However, the data might not be relevant for each of your model driven applications. Let's say that an organization has created two model driven applications, Fundraiser, and Innovation. In the fundraiser application, you would likely need details related to fundraising efforts such as an account's tax exemption status. However, it's likely that in the innovation application, you would not need that need that data. As a result, you would typically have two different account forms. One for the fundraising app with the tax exemption status details, and another for the innovation app without those fields.

It is possible to include multiple forms and views per table. In the screenshot, we're including multiple views to help manage donations. Only the selected forms will be displayed. However, if you do not select any view or forms, the system assumes that all items should be included in your app.

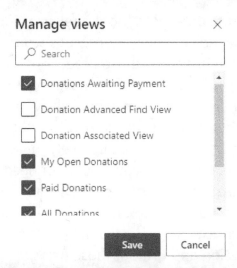

Add new content to an application

New content is added to the application by selecting the **Add** page button. When you add a new page, you specify which type of page you want to use.

There are three options to choose from:

> - **Table based form and view:** Display records of table in a full-page list view. Forms associated with that table are also included.
> - **Dashboard:** Displays charts and tables from multiple entities to visualize data on a single page. Multiple dashboards can be added to a model application.

> ➤ **Custom:** Allows you to design and build the type of page you want by dragging interactive components into the canvas.

Testing the application

By selecting the **Play** button on the top right, the app is put into **Play mode**. You can see the app that displays data based on the choices made in the design process.

Build a basic model-driven app

In this unit, you create a model-driven app by using one of the standard entities that are available in your Microsoft Power Apps environment.

Create a model-driven app

1. Sign in to <u>Power Apps</u> by using your organizational account.
2. Select the environment you want or go to the <u>Power Apps admin center</u> to create a new one.
3. On the **Home** page, select **Blank App**.
4. On the Create screen, select **Blank app based on Dataverse**, and click **Create**.

5. On the **New model-driven app** page, enter a **name** and **description** for the app. (For example, enter "My first app" for the name, and "This is my first model-driven application" for the description.)
6. After a few minutes, your new app will appear.

Add Account table to your app

You can add pages to your app by using the App Designer.

1. If necessary, using the navigation on the left, select the **show or hide menu names button** (looks like 3 horizontal lines) to show the menu names.
2. Select the **Group1** text. On the right-hand side of the screen change the Title to **Customers**.

3. Using the command bar at the top, select the **+ Add Page** button.
4. On the Add Page screen, select **Table based view and form,** then select the **Next** button.
5. On the Add table view and form pages screen, select **Account** then select the **Add** button.

Note

Your environment may not contain an account table. If that's the case, you'll need to create one. Use the navigation on the left and select **Dataverse**, expand, and select **Tables** On the top action bar, select **New table**. In the form that appears, add in Account in the Display name field and **Save**.

Add forms and views to your appScreenshot of how to create an Account table

Now that we've added a table to our app, we're going to specify which Account forms and views should be used with the application.

1. Using the navigation on the left, select **Pages.**

2. Expand **Account** and select **Account** form.
3. On the right-hand side of the screen, select **Add form**.
4. From the list of Forms that appears, select **Account.**

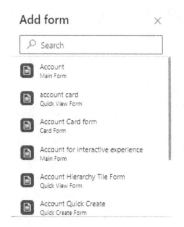

5. Under **Pages** on the left, select **Account** view.
6. On the right-hand side of the screen, select **Add view**.
7. Select the **My Active Accounts** view.
8. Select **Add view** again.
9. Select **Active Accounts**.
10. Select **Add view**.
11. Select **Inactive Accounts.**
    - o My Active Accounts
    - o Active Accounts
    - o Inactive Accounts

Add Contact page to your app

Next, we're going to add another table to our application. In this case, we are going to add the Contacts table since a customer could be either an account or a contact.

1. On the command bar at the top, select the **Add Page** button.
2. On the Add page screen, choose **table-based view and form**, then select the **Next** button.
3. In the **Search** field, enter **Contact**, then select the **Contact** table.
4. Select the **Add** button.

Save and publish your app

Now that you've successfully created your first model driven application, let's get ready to use it.

1. Using the command bar at the top select the **Save** button.
2. Once your application has been saved, select the **Publish** button.
3. To test your application, select the **Play** button.

GLOSSARY

Certainly! Here are some key terms related to building applications with Microsoft Power Apps:

1. **Canvas Apps:** Canvas Apps are Power Apps that allow users to create highly customizable and pixel-perfect applications. They provide a blank canvas where users can design the user interface and functionality using a wide range of controls, formulas, and connectors.

2. **Model-Driven Apps:** Model-Driven Apps are Power Apps that provide a data-centric approach to application development. They are built on top of the Common Data Service (CDS) and provide a pre-built data schema and user interface components, making it easier to create data-driven applications.

3. **Controls:** Controls in Power Apps are visual elements that allow users to interact with the application. They include buttons, forms, galleries, labels, input fields, and more. Controls can be customized with properties and formulas to define their behavior and appearance.

4. **Screen:** A screen is a visual container in a Power App where users can design and define a specific user interface. Power Apps typically consist of multiple screens that users can navigate through.

5. **Data Sources:** Data sources in Power Apps are the external systems or services from which the application retrieves and stores data. This can include databases, SharePoint lists, Excel files, Microsoft Dataverse, and various connectors to other services.

6. **Formulas:** Formulas in Power Apps are expressions used to define the behavior and logic of the application. They allow users to perform calculations, manipulate data, control the visibility of elements, and create conditional workflows.

7. **Connectors:** Connectors in Power Apps enable integration with external systems,

services, and data sources. They provide pre-built connectivity options for services like Microsoft 365, SharePoint, Dynamics 365, and various third-party applications.

8. *App Templates:* App Templates are pre-built application templates provided by Microsoft that can be customized to meet specific business needs. They serve as a starting point for app development and offer ready-to-use functionality and design elements.

9. *Publishing and Sharing:* Once an application is built with Power Apps, it can be published and shared with users within the organization or even externally. Power Apps supports various deployment options, including sharing within Microsoft Teams, SharePoint, or as standalone applications.

10. *App Lifecycle Management:* App Lifecycle Management refers to the process of managing and governing applications built with Power Apps throughout their lifecycle. This includes version control, testing, deployment, and ongoing maintenance and updates.

QUESTION AND ANSWERS

Q: What are Canvas Apps in Microsoft Power Apps, and how do they work? A: Canvas Apps in Microsoft Power Apps allow users to create highly customizable applications. They provide a blank canvas where users can design the user interface and functionality using a wide range of controls, formulas, and connectors. Users can drag and drop controls onto the canvas, customize their properties, and use formulas to define their behavior. Canvas Apps offer flexibility in design and can integrate with various data sources and services to create tailored applications.

Q: What are Model-Driven Apps in Microsoft Power Apps, and how do they differ from Canvas Apps? A: Model-Driven Apps in Microsoft Power Apps provide a data-centric approach to application development. They are built on top of the Common Data Service (CDS) and offer a pre-built data schema and user interface components. Unlike Canvas Apps, where the user interface is fully customizable, Model-Driven Apps provide a structured layout with pre-defined forms, views, and navigation. Users can configure the data model, business rules, and user experience, making it easier to create data-driven applications with consistent design and functionality.

Q: How do you add controls to a Power App, and what can they be used for? A: In Power Apps, controls are visual elements that users can add to their applications to interact with data and perform specific actions. Controls can be added by dragging and dropping them onto the canvas or form. Examples of controls include buttons, input fields, labels, galleries, and forms. Controls can be customized with properties and formulas to define their behavior, such as capturing user input, displaying data, or triggering actions.

Q: What are data sources in Power Apps, and how do they connect to external systems? A: Data sources in Power Apps are the external systems or services from which the application retrieves and stores data. Power Apps supports a wide range of data sources, including databases, SharePoint lists, Excel files, Microsoft Dataverse (formerly Common Data Service), and various connectors to other services like Salesforce or Dynamics 365. Users can connect to these data sources using connectors, which provide pre-built connectivity options and allow users to access, manipulate, and update data within the Power App.

Q: What are formulas in Power Apps, and how are they used? A: Formulas in Power Apps are expressions used to define the behavior and logic of the application. They enable users to perform calculations, manipulate data, control the visibility of elements, and create conditional workflows. Power Apps uses a formula language called Power Apps formula language (also known as Power Fx) that is similar to Excel formulas. Users can write formulas to set the values of properties, validate user input, filter data, and perform various other operations within the application.

Q: How can Power Apps be shared and published with users? A: Power Apps offers multiple options for sharing and publishing applications. Users can share their apps with others within their organization or even externally. Apps can be shared directly within Microsoft Teams, embedded within SharePoint sites, or published as standalone applications accessible through a URL. Power Apps also allows for role-based access control, allowing users to specify who can view, edit, or run the published applications.

Q: What is App Lifecycle Management in Power Apps, and why is it important? A: App Lifecycle Management in Power Apps refers to the process of managing and governing applications throughout their lifecycle, including development, testing, deployment, and ongoing maintenance. It involves version control, ensuring proper testing and quality assurance, managing changes and updates, and maintaining the security and performance of the applications. App Lifecycle Management is important to ensure the smooth operation of Power Apps solutions and to align with the organization's overall IT governance and best practices.

QUESTIONS

Certainly! Here are questions specifically focusing on building applications with Microsoft Power Apps:

1. What are Canvas Apps in Microsoft Power Apps, and how do they work?
2. What are Model-Driven Apps in Microsoft Power Apps, and how do they differ from Canvas Apps?
3. How do you add controls to a Power App, and what can they be used for?
4. What are data sources in Power Apps, and how do they connect to external systems?
5. What are formulas in Power Apps, and how are they used?
6. How can Power Apps be shared and published with users?
7. What is App Lifecycle Management in Power Apps, and why is it important?

CHAPTER 4

BUILDING AUTOMATION WITH MICROSOFT POWER AUTOMATE

Exam PL-900

Power Automate is used to automate repetitive business processes. Beyond simple workflows, Power Automate can send reminders on past due tasks, move business data between systems on a schedule, talk to more than 900 data sources or any publicly available API, and can even automate tasks on your local computer like computing data in Excel. All of this can be done by all skill levels, from typical business users to IT using Power Platform.

- ➤ Examine the capabilities of Power Automate
- ➤ Explore the different Power Automate apps
- ➤ Examine the components of a cloud flow
- ➤ Examine Power Automate scenarios
- ➤ Build a basic cloud flow
- ➤ Build a basic desktop flow
- ➤ Examine the business value provided by Power Automate

The capabilities of Power Automate

Do you find yourself regularly downloading email attachments and then uploading the file to the database? Every business in every industry has repetitive tasks that impact their organization. The process of getting a new purchase order approved might involve taking a form from your desk to get it approved. An employee might need to log into a website every morning to find daily numbers and then save those numbers into another system. Not only can repetitive processes like these be time consuming, but they can also be prone to errors. If someone mis-enters something, it could result in a missed deadline or a financial loss.

Microsoft Power Automate is about having computers manage repetitive tasks. It gives anyone with the knowledge of the business process to create a repeatable flow that when triggered, leaps into action and performs the process.

Common scenarios and capabilities of Power Automate:

> **Automating repetitive** tasks such as moving data from one system to another.
> Guiding a user through a process so they can complete the different stages. For example, a sales organization might want to guide sellers through the process of selling products to customers.
> **Automating desktop** based and website processes with robotic process automation (RPA) capabilities. For example, a user working at a bank needs to update the exchange rates daily. That user would utilize RPA to login to the website from which they get the rates, save the exchange rates to their desktop, and then update them in a company spread sheet.

Exam PL-900

Microsoft Power Automate works by creating flows. These flows are then used to do things such as interact with different systems, guide users through a process, or make users more productive by automating daily tasks.

There are three primary types of Power Automate flows:

> **Business process flows**: These flows are used in model-driven apps to help people get work done. They provide a streamlined user experience that leads people through the processes their organization has defined for interactions that need to be advanced to a conclusion of some kind.

> **Cloud flows**: These are the most used flows. Cloud flows begin with a trigger such as receiving an email from a specific person, or a mention of your company in social media. Once triggered, they also generally include one or more actions such as creating a record in a different system or sending an approval request to someone.

> **Desktop flows** - These robotic process automation (RPA) flows allow you to record yourself performing actions on your desktop or within a web browser. You can then trigger a flow to perform that process for you. You can also pass data in or get data out of the process,

letting you automate even "manual" business processes.

Business process flows

Business process flows are mostly used in model-driven applications to help users get work done. They typically represent a process that a user follows through to completion. They provide a streamlined user experience to provide them with the best way to advance to a conclusion of some kind.

Some common scenarios where organizations might use business process flows are:

> **Sales Process:** Organizations can create sales focused business process flows that guide sellers through the entire sales process ensuring that they are following the organization proven sales procedures for maximizing their chance of winning the deal.
> **Case Resolution:** Support centers might create service centered business process flows that guide agents through the process of creating a case, troubleshooting the case, and ultimately resolving the case.
> **Event Planning:** An event planning company might use a business process flows to ensure that they are not missing a step when they are planning an event. Stages in the process can

exist for booking the venue, planning the meal, defining entertainment details and more.

> **Selling a home:** A real estate company might use a business process flow to assist their agents in getting a home ready for an open house. This might include having stages for capturing inspection details, staging the property, and coordinating with staff to ensure someone is available at the time.

In the image, we can see an example of a business process flow that's used to help guide an agent through the process of fielding an offer from a potential buyer.

During each stage, there is information that needs to be logged. Based on the information captured, the stages of the business process flow might change. For example, since the **Counter Offer** field is set to yes, the counter offer stage appears. If the **Counter Offer** field was set to no, the stage would not appear.

Cloud flows

As stated, cloud flows are the most common Power Automate flows. Cloud flows use connectors to interact with different services. Currently there are over 900 prebuilt connectors available. These connectors allow you to interact with data from other Microsoft products and data from non-Microsoft vendors such as Google, Salesforce, Oracle, and more.

There are three main types of cloud flows that you can create:

> **Automated flows:** These flows are automatically triggered by an event. This might be the arrival of an email from a specific person, or a mention of your company in social media. These are the most used cloud flow.

> **Instant flows:** These flows are started automatically and are done with the click of a button. You can automate for repetitive tasks from your Desktop or Mobile devices. For example, you might use an instant flow to instantly send a reminder to the team with the push of a button from your mobile device.

> **Scheduled:** These flows run on a defined schedule. They might be used to fire off daily data uploads to Microsoft SharePoint or a database.

Now that we have explored the types of cloud flows you can create, let's explore some common scenarios where organizations might use cloud flows.

> **Approvals:** They can be used to automate approval processes such as invoice approval, time off requests, project sign off, and more.
> **Application integration:** They can be used to allow an application to interact with another application. For example, a technician in the field might use a dedicated app to request a part. A Power Automate flow could automatically order the part in the company's inventory system.
> **Improve productivity:** End users might create personal Power Automate flows to automatically do things such as saving attachments received via email to specific locations like SharePoint or OneDrive for business.

More advanced examples of organizations utilizing Power Automate flows might include:

> Interfacing with a custom Application Programming Interface (API) built by a financial services company to automatically retrieve the most recent loan rates, and then calculate the rate of an individual based on their credit score.
> Create a smart data filing system whereas documents are received, and the content in them are scanned. Based on the type of document it is automatically filed in a specific location and could even be flagged as needed.

Since there are hundreds of templates available to support different scenarios, cloud flows can be easily created by anyone.

Desktop flows

Desktop flows are used to simulate user interaction with an application or a website. Desktop flows are often referred to as Robotic Process Automation (RPA). Think of it as a computer playing back tasks and steps that are otherwise done by an individual. In Power Automate, these types of flows are built using Power Automate for desktop. Desktop flows are different than cloud flows. A cloud flow performs an action based on API calls, whereas a desktop flow is like a macro as it is playing back previously recorded steps in order.

Some of the common scenarios where an organization might use desktop flows are:

> **Improve employee productivity:** A desktop flow can be created to replicate the actions of an end user who performs repetitive tasks. An example would be interacting with a specific website such as an interest rate site, and then entering that information into another application like an Excel Spreadsheet.

> **Interacting with a legacy system:** Many organizations are still using home built legacy applications that do not have modern APIs

Exam PL-900

available that could be used by a cloud flow. In these instances, you can still automate the interaction with the legacy application without needing to rebuild the application from the ground up.

> **Automating website interaction:** Many users need to interact with specific websites daily to enter details or capture information. For security reasons, many companies don't provide access to their APIs to allow you to do direct automation with their platform. A Desktop flow is a great way to mimic the user interaction and provide an automated solution.

> **Automate working with terminal emulation software:** Many organizations use terminal emulation software such as Citrix to reduce hardware cost. Users' login into simulated desktops. Many of these uses perform repetitive tasks. Desktop flows can be used to mimic user keystrokes and automate activity.

There are just some of the many different examples where an organization could use desktop flows. Let's look at another example. In this example, a real estate company uses a website to see if new properties have any environmental items attached to the property. If any are found, they take a screenshot of the report and log it into Excel. In this video, we show you how a desktop flow could automate this process after a new property is entered into their property management model-driven application.

Desktop flow

Many times, a desktop flow is part of a bigger overall automation solution. For example, an event management company provides different package tiers to their clients to help them with cost savings on their event. This means that clients do not need to pay separately for each service. The event management company pays the vendors on behalf of the client. For example, when they plan a wedding, they will book the venue, hire the caterer, book the entertainment, and even sometimes hire a florist. When the event is complete, each vendor will send them an invoice for the services they provided.

That process is as follows:

> ➢ Vendor invoices are received as email attachments in a dedicated email box.
> ➢ The invoice attachments are downloaded from the email and scanned to determine what the invoice is for. Details such as the vendor, invoice date, and invoice amount are extracted from the attachment.
> ➢ Based on the services provided, each invoice is sent to a specific person to be evaluated and either approved or denied.
> ➢ Individuals receive and interact with this request in Microsoft Teams.

> ➢ Once the invoice is approved, a new invoice is created in the event management companies legacy invoice application.
> ➢ Once entered and an invoice number is generated, a confirmation email that the invoice was processed is sent back to the vendor. This includes the invoice number.

The image shows a high-level breakdown of what this automation would look like in a Power Automate flow.

The whole process is done with a cloud flow.

1. The cloud flow is triggered automatically when an email is received in the dedicated mailbox in Outlook.
2. AI Builder is used to extract details from the invoice attachment such as the vendor, invoice date, and amount.
3. An approval request is sent to the appropriate person in Microsoft Teams. The request will include the invoice details that were extracted from the invoice.
4. Once the request is approved, the cloud flow will run a desktop flow that was

created to interact with the legacy application. The invoice details such as the vendor, invoice date, and amount are used in the creation of the invoice record.

5. Once the invoice is logged, the invoice number is captured and a new email is created in Outlook. The email includes the status of the invoice and the invoice number.

The different Power Automate apps

To ensure that Power Automate flow creators can create the flows and automations that they need, there are three different Power Automate applications that makers can use to create and manage the different types of flows available.

The primary applications are:

> **Power Automate Portal:** The maker portal provides a single access point for makers where they can easily create, manage, and monitor the different Power Automate flows they have created.

> **Power Automate Mobile:** Power Automate Mobile provides access to Power Automate functionality while on the go.

➤ **Power Automate for Desktop:** Power Automate Desktop is used to create robotic process automation flows.

Power Automate Portal

The easiest place to begin designing Power Automate flows is the Power Automate maker portal. The maker portal provides you with access to all the different elements that you can use with Power Automate. The image below shows what the Power Automate maker portal looks like.

When you first access the maker portal, the left navigation will be broken down into three sections:

1. The first section is related to creating and managing your Power Automate flows. It includes the following:

- ➢ **Home:** The main home screen for the maker portal. This provides you with quick access to many of the different Power Automate components in your tenant.
- ➢ **Create:** This is where you can create new Power Automate flows from.
- ➢ **Learn:** Provides access to multiple resources that you can use to help you improve your Power Automate skills.
- ➢ **My flows:** Provides access to all the Power Automate flows that you have created.

2. The second section provides access to different Power Automate elements that you can use with Power Automate such as AI Builder, Process Advisor, Connections and more. Items that would be available in this section include:

- ➢ **Approvals:** Provides access to any approvals that have been sent or received by you.
- ➢ **Connectors:** Used to connect to different sources that you want involved in the Automation you are creating.
- ➢ **Data:** Provides access to the data that is supporting your flows such as Dataverse tables, gateways, and customer connectors.
- ➢ **Monitor:** Provides analytics around the different flows.

➢ **AI Builders:** Provides access to AI Builder tools that can be used as part of a Power Automate solution.
➢ **Process Advisor:** Provides tools that organizations can use to analyze organizational process to identify scenarios where automation could be used to support an organization.
➢ **Solutions:** Provides access to the different solutions that have been deployed to your environment.

> The items in this section can be pinned and un-pinned to the navigation to ensure that only the elements that you want to display will be shown.

3. The finial section provides easy access to additional Power Platform sites that can be useful. The items available here include:

➢ Power Platform admin center
➢ Power Apps maker portal
➢ Power Pages maker portal
➢ Power Virtual Agent portal
➢ Power BI

Power Automate mobile

There are many different scenarios where individuals may need access to Power Automate from their mobile device. For example, a manager may need to approve a change order that has been submitted for an upcoming project. Until approved, the project remains in a holding pattern which could eat into the company's profits.

The Power Automate mobile application is available for both Android and IOS devices. It provides users with the familiar look and feel of Power Automate while they are on the go.

With the Power Automate mobile application, you can:

> **Run instant flows:** Any instant flow that you have created will be available here. Selecting the flow will run it.
> **Manage activities:** Provides easy access to any items that require your approval as well as any notifications.
> **Create new flows:** New cloud flows can be created directly from within the application.
> **Manage Existing flows:** Easily monitor and make changes to any cloud flows that you have created.

Power Automate for Desktop

Power Automate for Desktop flows broaden the existing capabilities in Power Automate and enable you to automate all repetitive desktop processes. The Power Automate desktop flow designer contains prebuilt drag-and-drop actions that can be easily inserted into a flow.

Desktop flows are addressed to essentially everyone who is performing simple or complex rule-based tasks on their workstations. Users at home, small businesses, enterprises, or larger companies can use automation capabilities in Power Automate to create flows, interact with everyday tools like email and Excel, or work with modern and legacy applications.

Examples of simple and complex tasks you can automate are:

> ➤ Quickly organize your documents using dedicated files and folders actions
> ➤ Accurately extract data from websites and store them in Excel files using web and Excel automation
> ➤ Apply desktop automation capabilities to put your work on autopilot

If you are a home user who is accessing a weather website to see tomorrow's forecast or a self-employed businessperson extracting information from vendors' invoices or even an employee of a large enterprise who automates data entry on an ERP system, Power Automate is designed for you.

It allows you to automate legacy applications, such as terminal emulators, modern web and desktop applications, Excel files, and folders. You can interact with the machine using application UI elements, images, or coordinates.

Exam PL-900

The components of a cloud flow

As you begin to create Power Automate flows, it's important to note that every cloud flow has two main parts.

> **Trigger:** Determine what starts the flow
> **Actions:** Determine what the flow does

Triggers

Triggers are the starting action for a flow. A trigger could be something such as a new email arriving in your inbox or a new item being added to a SharePoint list. A flow only has one trigger.

While a flow only has one trigger, there are a few different types of triggers that can be used:

> **When something changes:** This type of trigger runs when data is changed. It could be a new item created in SharePoint, when a lead is updated in Dynamics, or when an event has been deleted from Outlook for example. **When something changes** triggers are the most used triggers.
> **On a schedule:** You can set up a flow to be triggered at a certain time of day and with a

recurrence. This scheduling allows for processes such as checking every day at 8 AM to see if there are account renewals pending and if so, sending an email to the necessary people.

> **On a button press:** This trigger takes shape in many ways. It can be when a flow virtual button is run through the mobile app an. a physical button is clicked with third party options. Alternatively, it can be when a button is pressed inside of Power Apps. This capability gives you and/or the users control to "run" a flow on demand.

Actions

Actions are what you want to happen when a trigger is invoked. For example, the new email trigger starts the action of creating a new file on OneDrive for Business. A typical Power Automate flow has multiple actions.

Now that we have introduced you to triggers and actions, let's examine how they are used together when you create a flow. In this example we will examine purchase order approval. Approvals are often processes that are done manually but could easily be done with a Power Automate flow.

Using Microsoft Power Apps, an organization can easily create a purchase request app. Users who need to purchase something would initiate the purchase order process by going into the Purchase Order Power App creating a purchase order (PO) request. In those instances, the trigger would be the user selecting a submit button on the power app. Once the request is submitted, the information is sent to a Power Automate flow.

This is where the actions come in. The flow's first action is to identify the manager of the user who initiated the PO request. In this case, the flow is using a Microsoft 365 connector to retrieve the user's manager automatically from Azure AD. Next it creates an approval request in Microsoft Teams. The approval request is assigned to the manager who was identified in the Get manager action.

The image shows an example of the starting point of the flow:

Many times, organizations have different procedures to support different types of scenarios. For example, a company might have a policy where purchase requests for more than $10,000.00 need to be sent to a Vice President before they can be completed. This logic can be easily built into a flow using conditions. In this case, after the manager receives the approval request and approves it, the flow includes a condition to see if the value of the request is for more than $10,000.00. If it is, there's another action to send an approval to the VP in Microsoft Teams. If the item is less than $10,000.00, then the item is officially approved and the request is submitted.

The image provides a high-level example of what that flow may look like.

Even though this flow has many decision points, each of the decisions is handled without needing to write any code. Once the flow is activated, it handles purchase order requests automatically. The approval process will become part of your users' daily activities.

Work with your data where it lives

When building or creating any type of automation, access to your data is important. Without correct access to the data, the automation may not be able to execute appropriately. Power Automate makes connecting to your data easy with over 900 connectors that you can use to easily connect to data and services across the web and on-premises.

Some common data sources include:

➢ Microsoft Dataverse

- ➤ Salesforce
- ➤ Dynamics 365
- ➤ Google Drive
- ➤ Office 365
- ➤ Oracle

As you see from the previous example, you don't have to choose just one data source. Microsoft Power Platform easily supports multiple data connections allowing you to bring data together from many platforms into a single automation.

Now that we've seen how a Power Automate flow works, let's examine some different scenarios where organizations might use Power Automate flows with other services.

Consider Power Automate scenarios

Most organizations utilize multiple applications and services every day. Users are sending and receiving emails in one application, while salespeople and service reps might be working in the organization's Customer Relationship Management (CRM) System. Having so many different applications, it is extremely common to have processes or procedures that need to pass information across these applications.

Exam PL-900

One of the many advantages of Power Automate is how easily it works with the different applications that organizations use each day. This is true even when the applications are not built from the same vendor. For example, using connectors, you can easily trigger a flow when an order is created in Salesforce and store a copy of it in SharePoint. Regardless of which services and applications an organization is using, there are many times when a flow will be interacting with many of the most popular Microsoft technologies. This could be triggering a flow when someone creates a new document in Microsoft SharePoint or sends an approvals card to a manager in Microsoft Teams. Power Automate can easily be used to create processes around interact with those applications.

Let's examine some use-cases related to popular Microsoft technologies.

Use flows with approvals

We have mentioned approvals a few times throughout this module. Whether you need written acknowledgment from a manager or a formal authorization from a diverse group of stakeholders, getting things approved is part of almost every organization.

With the approvals capability in Power Automate, you can automate sign-off requests and combine human decision making into workflows. When you submit an approval in a flow, approvers are notified and can review and act on the request.

Some popular cases where approvals can be used include:

> **Approving vacation time requests:** Employees can submit a vacation request via a dedicated application, or by filling out a vacation request form. The request is sent to a manager who can approve or deny the request.
> **Approving documents that need sign off:** Documents that require approval or signing off can be easily sent to the appropriate person to be signed off on. Once approved, a confirmation or copy of the signed document could be sent to all parties to confirm it was completed.
> **Approving expense reports:** After filling out an expense report, a Power Automate flow can identify the person's manager, and send them the report for their approval.

Power Automate and Microsoft SharePoint

Microsoft SharePoint is a popular application that allows organizations to create sites where users can share documents and information with colleagues, partners, and customers. With the document management capabilities of SharePoint, users can easily track different versions of documents, and collaborate with others. With SharePoint being used to support so many different scenarios, it makes sense that organizations would want to be able to automate many of the different elements.

Let's look at some different examples of how you can use Power Automate with SharePoint:

Managing approval flows

There are multiple ways that Power Automate could be used to support approval processes in SharePoint. For example, documents that contain sensitive information such as personal details, financial details, or strategies often require approval. With the content approval feature in SharePoint, you can put a simple approval process for documents in a specific document library. Using this content approval process, documents pending approval will not be visible to users until they are approved. This prevents documents that do not meet organizational standards accidentally being used which could result in financial losses.

Another example is related to SharePoint sites. Organizations will often create SharePoint team sites that connect team members with shared content and resources. As users create different pages within a site, organizations may want to initiate an approval process to make sure that the page content is accurate, appropriate, and meets the organizational standards for content. SharePoint can be easily configured to require that changes to a site be approved before they go live.

Working with files and lists

There are many scenarios where Power Automate flows can be used with SharePoint files and lists. One example is using Power Automate flows to help manage permissions of an individual item in a list or a file that is stored in a document library. For example, a flow could be used to grant access or provide approval for when an item is created or added to a specific folder. When an item is created, an approval request is created. Once the request is received, the flow will send the request to a manager who could approve the request.

Additionally, Power Automate flows could be used to create SharePoint items based on actions occurring in other applications, such as an invoice being created in an ERP application. For example, one an invoice is created, the Power Automate flow could save the invoice as a PDF, and then save the file to a dedicated customer folder in a SharePoint document library.

Using Power Automate with Microsoft Outlook

Microsoft Outlook is the most widely used email application in businesses. Users not only use it for sending and receiving email, but they also use it for managing their individual contacts as well as managing their daily activities. This provides many different opportunities where Power Automate could potentially be used to automate Outlook scenarios. For example, a real estate agent might create and store customer contracts in popular document services such as Dropbox, OneDrive, or SharePoint. Once a customer contract is created, a Power Automate flow could automatically create an email to the customer and attach the newly created contracts as attachments. Additionally, once the customer sends back the signed contract, another flow could save the signed contracts back to the document repository. This helps the real estate agent ensure that contracts are being sent out and cataloged in a timely manner, with no manual steps needing to be taken by the agent.

Since scenarios similar to this occur daily in most organizations, two of the most popular connectors used in flows to send or receive email are the Outlook.com connector, which is used for personal email scenarios, and the Office 365 Outlook connector, which is used for business scenarios. Both connectors offer similar operations that you can use to manage your mail, calendars, and contacts. You can perform actions such as send mail, schedule meetings, add contacts, and more with either of these connectors.

Using flows with Microsoft Forms

Microsoft Forms is an online survey creator that lets individuals and businesses easily create surveys and polls for things such as capturing customer feedback, measuring employee satisfaction, or organizing team events. There are many instances where forms or polls created with Microsoft Forms could benefit from automation. For example, more and more schools are leveraging Microsoft Forms to support scenarios such as student quizzes. A teacher could use a flow that would notify them when a student turns in a quiz. A real-estate organization might use Microsoft Forms for new clients to provide details about themselves and the types of properties they are interested in. With a Power Automate flow, after a potential client completes the form, an email notification could be sent to an agent in their area. This ensures that the agent reaching out to the customer is local and ensures that the agent can engage with the customer as soon as possible.

There are multiple templates available to assist flow creators in building flow to support different Microsoft Forms scenarios, such as starting an approval process based on a form submission or tracking Microsoft Forms responses in Microsoft Excel.

In the Image below, we filtered the list to only display templates that work with Microsoft Forms. We were able to take it one step further and search for templates that work with Outlook. The list of templates shows only templates that include Microsoft Forms and Outlook.

Using flows with Microsoft Teams

Microsoft Teams is a powerful messaging and collaboration tool that organizations all over the world use to provide their employees with a workspace for real-time collaboration and communication, running meeting events or trainings, and for sharing applications and files.

Power Automate flows can be used in three scenarios with Teams:

> - **Trigger** flows from Teams messages: In this scenario, you can create flows that are triggered when someone selects a Teams message. The flow can then run like any other flow you create.
> - **Use flows with** adaptive cards: Here, adaptive cards can be used as the trigger for flows. A full set of rich adaptive cards is available to you.
> - **Create flows from within the** Power Apps app in Teams: Use the Power Apps app in Teams to create flows that use Dataverse for Teams. Dataverse for Teams is a built-in, low-code data platform for Teams that empowers users to build custom apps and workflows within Teams by using Power Apps and Power Automate.

Exam PL-900

Build a basic Power Automate cloud flow

Now that we've reviewed the primary elements of Power Automate, let's take a high-level look at how to create a basic Power Automate cloud flow.

It can be time-consuming to search for attachments through email at Contoso Manufacturing. To alleviate those time-consuming searches, you can build a flow that stores email attachments in different folders on your Microsoft OneDrive for Business account. Thankfully, there's a template to help you get started.

Cloud flows can quickly be created from the Power Automate maker portal. You can either select the **+ Create** button on the screen or select **+ Create** from the left navigation.

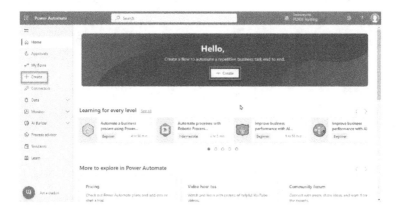

The next thing you must decide is whether you apply one of the many different templates available to create your flow or build your own from scratch. As you become more advanced, you might want to build your own, but when you are first starting, the easiest way is to start with a template.

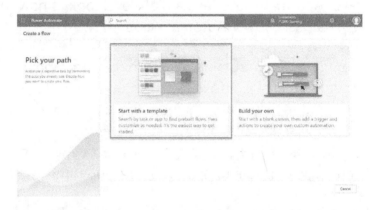

Initially you see a series of predefined filters that you can select from. These are populated based on past things you've done. You can select one of the predefined filters, or you can search by a specific word or phrase like "Outlook". When you select a specific template, you see details about the template, including the data sources it connects to.

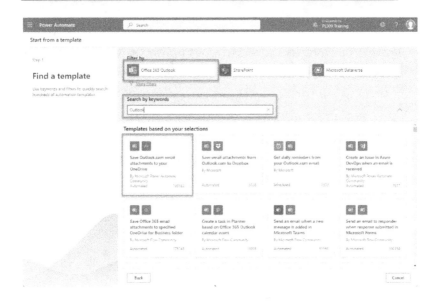

Once the initial flow is created, you need to enter details to ensure the flow operates as intended. For example, if you want to store email attachments in different OneDrive folders based on who sent you the email, you need to configure the condition accordingly. In the image, we see that any attachments are saved to a OneDrive folder called Power Apps.

Exam PL-900

For the flow we just discussed, the folder where we want to save the attachments is the only piece of data we need to provide. Everything is done with a point and click interface. As you become more familiar with Power Automate, you may decide that you want to create your flows from scratch to support more advanced scenarios.

Once your flow has been created, you can save it by selecting the **Save** button.

Now that we've walked you through the steps of a building a flow, let's see the process in action. In the following simulation, we create a simple flow from a template that saves email attachments to a specific OneDrive for business folder based on who the email was from.

Click-through demo: Build a Power Automate cloud flow

In this click-through demonstration, you are guided through the process of building a cloud flow.

Build a cloud flow

Build a Desktop flow

While cloud flows are executed in the cloud using connectors to attach to APIs, desktop flows run on a local machine. Power Automate for Desktop is an application installed on your computer and it records Power Automate desktop flows running directly on the machine. Once created, desktop flows can be triggered manually or by cloud flows. For example, a desktop flow that automates a user's interaction with an excel spreadsheet might be triggered manually. A desktop flow that creates an invoice is typically triggered automatically, since invoice details would likely come for somewhere else.

Let's take a high-level look at the process for creating a desktop flow automation.

Desktop flows are created using the Power Automate for Desktop application. This is an application that is installed on the computer where the desktop flow is performing the operation.

Like cloud flows, there are multiple desktop flow templates that you can use to help get started building desktop flows. These templates are available in the **Examples** section. Examples are broken down into common scenarios.

In the image, you see a screenshot of the Desktop Automation examples. Examples range from beginner to advanced.

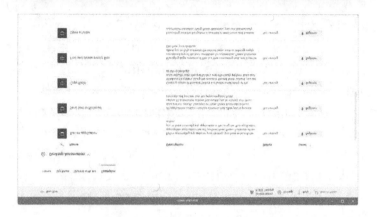

Once you are ready to work with one of the examples, such as the flow that will open a file. You want to copy the original to ensure you don't modify the original.

Creating desktop flows in done in the Power Automate Desktop designer.

The designer is laid out as follows:

1. **Toolbar:** Contains basic operations for use with actions, such asSave, Undo, Copy, Debug and Paste. Also contains buttons to start the UI/Web recorders and to control the process execution, such as Start, Pause and Stop.

2. **Sub flows:** Allows you to create sub flows under your main flow.
3. **Actions pane:** Contains all Power Automate Desktop Actions and includes a search bar that assists in finding specific actions by matching the action name to the text string.
4. **Workspace:** Contains all the actions added to the process so far. Functions are separated into tabs.
5. **Input/output variables:** Contains all the variables you created in the process.
6. **Flow variables:** List variables created by the process.

This flow will assist a user in opening files. It opens a file dialog box where the user can select a specific file to open. Once you select the file, it opens. It's a basic example but it does help to illustrate desktop flow concepts well.

You can add more actions by expanding an action category, selecting the action you want and then dragging the action into the workspace. In the image, we have expanded the Excel group to display a list of Excel actions. If we want a flow to open a specific excel spread sheet, we select the Launch Excel action.

Another way to add actions is to use the recorder. The recorder lets you record the steps that you execute inside websites, on the desktop, or inside applications. As you perform actions such as opening an application and filling out data, the recorder keeps track of the steps you performed. Once you can complete the operation you want, those steps stored and saved. The steps can then be easily edited inside the designer.

As you're building a desktop flow, you want to test it to ensure that it is performing as intended. You can test your flow at any time by selecting the **Run** button. The recorded steps are played back in the order they were defined in the flow. In the image, the flow is displaying an open file dialog where the user can select the file to open.

Once created, this desktop flow can be run manually by an individual user by selecting it in their Power Automate for Desktop app, or automatically by being triggered by a cloud flow. In the image, you can see an example of manually running a desktop flow from the Power Automate for Desktop application.

Now that we've walked through the high-level steps to create a desktop flow, let's demonstrate the process. In the following click-through demonstration, we create a desktop flow that opens an invoice application and creates a new invoice.

Click-through demo: Build a Power Automate desktop flow

In this click-through demonstration, you're guided through the process of building a desktop flow.

Build a desktop flow

Build a basic Power Automate flow

In the following exercise, you create an instant flow that is used to send you a reminder in 1 minute.

Task 1 – Create the Flow

1. In a browser window, navigate to https://make.powerautomate.com.
2. On the home screen, select the **+Create** button.
3. On the **Pick your Path** screen, select **Start with a Template**.
4. In the **Search by Keywords** section, enter the text "button", and press **Enter**.
5. Locate and select the **Send myself a reminder in 10 minutes** flow.

6. In the name field, enter the text, **remind me in 1 minute**.
7. Select the **Next** button.
8. In the **Delay** step, change the **Count** field to **1** minute.
9. In the **Send a push notification step**, enter the following text into the **Text** field. **Here is your 1-minute reminder "Your First name".**
10. Select the **Save** button.

Task 2 – Test your Flow

In this next task, we use the Power Automate mobile application to trigger the reminder.

1. If you do not already have the **Power Automate mobile** application installed on your device, download the app from your device's app store.
2. Once downloaded, sign into the mobile application using your credentials.
3. Select the **Account** Icon at the bottom of the app.
4. In the **Environment** section, switch to the environment you created the flow button in.
5. Select **OK**.
6. Once everything loads, select the **Button** Icon at the bottom of your app.

7. Select the **Remind me in 1 minute** button.
8. After 1 minute, you receive a push notification on your mobile device.

The business value of Power Automate

You now have an overview of Power Automate and how it drives business value. Now we explore how TruGreen is improving customer experience by incorporating chat bots, artificial intelligence, and Microsoft Power Platform.

TruGreen embarks on an all-up digital transformation.

As part of TruGreen's commitment to providing customers with what they need to "live life outside", they teamed up with Microsoft. One step toward that goal was incorporating Microsoft Power Platform, including Power Automate, to provide proactive and predictive services to their customers.

Below you can see an infographic of their digital transformation strategy:

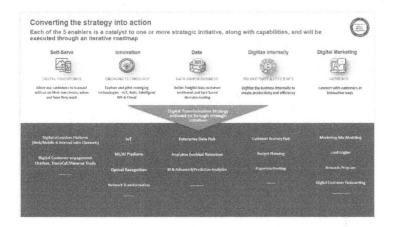

Converting the strategy into action
Each of the 5 enablers is a catalyst to one or more strategic initiative, along with capabilities, and will be executed through an iterative roadmap

To provide better services, they built a new artificial intelligence enabled virtual agent bot. The virtual agent was built without writing any code. Instead, it used Power Virtual Agents to facilitate handling routine customer requests and to act based on customer intent. To expose and interact with the back-end data required, they used Power Automate.

TruGreen used some of the hundreds of connectors available for Microsoft Power Platform to connect to traditional data sources. Using these capabilities, they had their first prototype running in two days, once again without a single line of code.

In addition, they had systems that didn't have APIs available to the connectors. For these systems, they used desktop flows. With desktop flows, they were able to mimic onscreen actions that customer service associates used to perform manually via robotic process automation (RPA).

Now they have a fully functional virtual agent for interacting with their customers that can act on the customers' intent in a meaningful way. This is just the first step as they continue to drive better customer experiences and more business value using these tools.

To read more about the virtual agents TruGreen has built and what they have planned next, see the full case study <u>here</u>.

Now you have an overview of Power Automate and how TruGreen has used this powerful service. The demo video shows a couple of types of flows and how to get started with Power Automate yourself.

Watch this video to see a demo of Power Automate.

GLASSARY

Certainly! Here are some key terms related to building automation with Microsoft Power Automate:

1. ***Flow:*** A flow in Microsoft Power Automate represents an automated workflow that connects different systems, services, and actions. It consists of triggers, conditions, actions, and connectors that define the sequence and logic of the automation.

2. **Trigger:** A trigger is an event that starts the execution of a flow. It can be a specific action, such as receiving an email, creating a new record in a database, or a scheduled time-based event. Triggers initiate the flow and define when and how it should run.

3. **Actions:** Actions are the individual steps within a flow that perform specific tasks. Actions can include sending emails, creating or updating records, making HTTP requests, applying data transformations, or performing calculations. Multiple actions can be combined to create complex automation scenarios.

4. **Connectors:** Connectors in Power Automate are pre-built integrations that enable communication and data exchange between different systems and services. They provide a standardized way to connect to various applications, databases, cloud services, and APIs. Connectors offer a wide range of actions and triggers specific to the connected service.

5. **Conditions:** Conditions in Power Automate are used to create branching logic within a flow. They allow you to define if-then scenarios based on specific criteria. Conditions evaluate data or properties and determine which path the flow should follow based on the outcome.

6. **Expressions:** Expressions are used in Power Automate to manipulate data, perform calculations, and create dynamic values. They are based on the Power Fx formula language, which is similar to Excel formulas. Expressions can be used in actions, conditions, and variables to transform and manipulate data during the flow execution.

7. **Loops:** Loops in Power Automate allow you to iterate over a collection of items or perform repetitive actions. They enable you to process multiple records, apply the same set of actions to each item, and automate tasks that involve working with lists or arrays of data.

8. **Variables:** Variables in Power Automate are used to store and manipulate data within a flow. They allow you to store values temporarily, perform calculations,

or hold intermediate results. Variables can be assigned values, updated, and used in expressions to control the flow's behavior.

9. ***Approval:*** Approval actions in Power Automate allow you to create automated approval processes within your flows. They enable you to send approval requests to users or groups, track the status of approvals, and perform actions based on the approval outcome. Approval actions streamline and automate the review and decision-making processes.

10. ***Error Handling:*** Error handling in Power Automate involves managing and responding to errors that occur during the execution of a flow. It includes actions such as catching and handling exceptions, logging errors, sending notifications, and implementing retry or fallback mechanisms to ensure the flow can handle unexpected situations.

QUESTIONS AND ANSWERS

Q: What is a flow in Microsoft Power Automate?

A: In Microsoft Power Automate, a flow represents an automated workflow that connects different systems, services, and actions. It consists of triggers, actions, conditions, and connectors that define the sequence and logic of the automation.

Q: What is a trigger in Power Automate? A: A trigger is an event that initiates the execution of a flow in Power Automate. It can be a specific action, such as receiving an email, creating a new record in a database, or a scheduled time-based event. Triggers define when and how the flow should start.

Q: How do actions work in Power Automate? A: Actions in Power Automate are the individual steps within a flow that perform specific tasks. They can include sending emails, creating or updating records in a database, making HTTP requests, applying data transformations, or performing calculations. Actions are combined to create the desired automation scenario.

Q: What are connectors in Power Automate? A: Connectors in Power Automate are pre-built integrations that enable communication and data exchange between different systems and services. They provide a standardized way to connect to various applications, databases, cloud services, and APIs. Connectors offer a wide range of actions and triggers specific to the connected service.

Q: How are conditions used in Power Automate? A: Conditions in Power Automate are used to create branching logic within a flow. They allow you to define if-then scenarios based on specific criteria. Conditions evaluate data or properties and determine which path the flow should follow based on the outcome.

Q: What are expressions in Power Automate, and how are they used? A: Expressions in Power Automate are used to manipulate data, perform calculations, and create dynamic values. They are based on the Power Fx formula language, which is similar to Excel formulas. Expressions can be used in actions, conditions, and variables to transform and manipulate data during the flow execution.

Q: How do loops work in Power Automate? A: Loops in Power Automate allow you to iterate over a collection of items or perform repetitive actions. They enable you to process multiple records, apply the same set of actions to each item, and automate tasks that involve working with lists or arrays of data.

Q: What are variables in Power Automate, and how are they used? A: Variables in Power Automate are used to store and manipulate data within a flow. They allow you to store values temporarily, perform calculations, or hold intermediate results. Variables can be assigned values, updated, and used in expressions to control the flow's behavior.

Q: How can approval processes be automated with Power Automate? A: Power Automate provides approval actions that allow you to create automated approval processes within your flows. You can send approval requests to users or groups, track the status of approvals, and perform actions based on the approval outcome. Approval actions streamline and automate the review and decision-making processes.

Q: How is error handling implemented in Power Automate? A: Error handling in Power Automate involves managing and responding to errors that occur during the execution of a flow. It includes actions such as catching and handling exceptions, logging errors, sending notifications, and implementing retry or fallback mechanisms to ensure the flow can handle unexpected situations.

QUESTIONS

Certainly! Here are questions specifically focusing on building automation with Microsoft Power Automate:

1. What is a flow in Microsoft Power Automate?
2. What is a trigger in Power Automate and how does it initiate a flow?
3. How do actions work in Power Automate and what tasks can they perform?
4. What are connectors in Power Automate and what role do they play in the automation process?
5. How are conditions used in Power Automate to create branching logic?
6. What are expressions in Power Automate and how are they used to manipulate data?
7. How do loops work in Power Automate and what purpose do they serve in automation?
8. What are variables in Power Automate and how are they used to store and manipulate data?
9. How can approval processes be automated with Power Automate?
10. How is error handling implemented in Power Automate to manage and respond to errors?

Exam PL-900

Certainly! Here's a glossary of key terms related to the PL-900 exam, also known as the Microsoft Power Platform Fundamentals:

1. Power Platform: The suite of Microsoft tools and technologies consisting of Power Apps, Power Automate, Power BI, and Power Virtual Agents that enables users to create custom business applications, automate workflows, analyze data, and build chatbot experiences.

2. Power Apps: A low-code/no-code platform that allows users to build custom web and mobile applications without extensive coding knowledge.

3. Power Automate: A workflow automation platform that enables users to create automated processes, integrate applications and services, and streamline business workflows.

4. Power BI: A business intelligence tool that provides data visualization, interactive dashboards, and reporting capabilities to analyze and present data insights.

5. Power Virtual Agents: A tool for building intelligent chatbots without the need for coding, allowing businesses to provide automated and personalized conversational experiences.

6. Common Data Service (CDS): A cloud-based data storage and management service that provides a unified and secure data platform for storing and integrating data across the Power Platform.

7. Connectors: Pre-built integration points that allow Power Platform components to connect with external systems and services, facilitating data exchange and interoperability.

8. Solutions: Logical containers that group related Power Platform components, such as apps, flows,

dashboards, and entities, enabling easy packaging, deployment, and management of assets.

9. Data Connectors: Connectors specifically designed to connect Power Platform components with various data sources, allowing users to retrieve, manipulate, and synchronize data from external systems.

10. Data Modeling: The process of defining the structure, relationships, and business rules for organizing data within the Power Platform, typically using entities, fields, and relationships.

11. Power Platform Administration: Activities related to managing and securing the Power Platform environment, including user management, access control, security settings, and monitoring.

12. AI Builder: An artificial intelligence (AI) service within the Power Platform that enables users to easily add AI capabilities, such as form processing, object detection, and prediction, to their Power Apps and Power Automate workflows.

13. Power Platform Licensing: The various licensing plans and options available for the Power Platform, including Power Apps licensing, Power Automate licensing, Power BI licensing, and considerations for licensing models and pricing.

14. Power Platform Governance: Strategies and practices for ensuring proper usage, security, and compliance within the Power Platform environment, including data loss prevention, data privacy, and governance policies.

15. Power Platform Community: The community of users, developers, and experts who actively engage in discussions, share knowledge, provide support, and contribute to the growth of the Power Platform ecosystem.

www.ingramcontent.com/pod-product-compliance
Lightning Source LLC
La Vergne TN
LVHW051229050326
832903LV00028B/2315